Rebekah,

Live Your
Dreams !

Wendy McCaig

"McCaig's vision of Christian hospitality involves opening ourselves to the most vulnerable-the abused wife, the drug addict, the ex-felon, the abandoned elderly-and discovering there the presence of God. Friendships with those close at home-family and neighbors-as well as with those across racial and class lines illustrate how 'God never works alone.' This beautifully written book is a call to all of us to embrace our dreams, whether large and small, and in so doing respond to God's call to be Christ's body for the world."

> —Elizabeth Newman, author of *Untamed Hospitality: Welcoming God and Other Strangers*

"Years ago, God gave Joseph an unpopular but ultimately redemptive dream that altered the course of his nation. Today, God has spoken a dream of the same fabric to my friend and courageous leader Wendy McCaig. Those who are wise enough to listen to this dreamer will become a part of a movement of the Church Distributed and will touch their communities with grace and hope."

> —John P. Chandler, author of *Courageous Church Leadership: Conversations with Effective Practitioners*

FROM THE SANCTUARY TO THE STREETS

FROM THE SANCTUARY TO THE STREETS

How the Dreams of One City's Homeless Sparked
a Faith Revolution that Transformed a Community

WENDY R. McCAIG

CASCADE *Books* · Eugene, Oregon

FROM THE SANCTUARY TO THE STREETS
How the Dreams of One City's Homeless Sparked a Faith Revolution that
Transformed a Community

Cascade Books
An Imprint of Wipf and Stock Publishers
199 W. 8th Ave., Suite 3
Eugene, OR 97401

www.wipfandstock.com

ISBN 13: 978-1-60899-089-4

Cataloging-in-Publication data:

Wendy R. McCaig.
    From the sanctuary to the streets : how the dreams of one city's homeless sparked
a faith revolution that transformed a community / Wendy R. McCaig.

    ISBN 13: 978-1-60899-089-4

    x + 168 p.; 23 cm. Includes bibliographical references.

    1. Church work with the homeless. 2. Women—Religious Life. 3. Homeless
persons—Biography. 4. Homelessness—United States—Case Studies. 5.
Homelessness—Religious Aspects—Christianity. I. Title.

BV4456 .M30 2010

Manufactured in the U.S.A.

Dedicated to my wonderful husband, Chris,
and my three beautiful daughters, Caitlin, Kristen, and Caroline,
whose love and support made this book possible.

Contents

Acknowledgments

This book would not exist without the hundreds of homeless men and women in Richmond, Virginia, who chose to share what they had with others in need. It is their tireless service to their neighbors and their willingness to share their stories, friendship, and lives with me over the years that inspired me to share our collective story with the world. In addition, I stand in awe of the hundreds of volunteers who left their places of comfort and journeyed across cultural boundaries to build relationships with these urban saints. Together these cross-cultural missionaries have reminded me of the power of the practice of Christian hospitality that transforms not only the urban landscape but also suburban congregations that support this practice. Without the faithful service of the team (staff, board of directors, AmeriCorps members, and volunteers), Embrace Richmond would not exist, and I would not have had the privilege of going on the journey of discovery shared in this book.

I never would have persevered through the writing process without my editor, Ulrike Guthrie, whose faith in this project helped me see the value of sharing this story, and whose editorial contributions helped me uncover and articulate the power of this story. In addition to Ulrike's contributions, dozens of friends and family members invested hours reading, offering suggestions, and assisting with the editing process. I am particularly thankful for the contributions made by Colleen Kenny, a member of my initial writing-critique group. Colleen's thoughtful and thorough responses had a significant effect on the work's final shape.

The inspiration for and initial funding of much of the research for this book was provided by Valparaiso University's Practicing Our Faith grant program. I owe a debt of gratitude to Don C. Richter, associate director of the Valparaiso Project, and Dorothy C. Bass, director of the Valparaiso Project, who encouraged me to capture these stories and make them available to others.

1 Learning to Dream Again

The place God calls you to is the place where your deep gladness and the world's deep hunger meet.

—FREDERICK BUECHNER

As a child, I was a dreamer, one of those kids who could lie in the grass for hours staring at the clouds, finding elephants, trains, and castles there. But something happened to me when I got my first paycheck. I stopped dreaming and got sucked into some invisible machine. Like a hamster on a wheel, I raced faster and faster trying to reach an unknown destination that promised to be always just a few more steps ahead. So I kept sprinting—until one cold November day in 1997 when a sudden blow knocked me off that treadmill: a loss so disturbing that I cannot bring myself to share it with you just yet. The day it happened, I think my heart stopped, and I felt as though I had died. As I lay on the ground, unable to move, I stared up at the heavens and began to wonder, "What is the meaning of all this? Is this all there is to life?"

That inquisitive girl of my youth slowly returned and began to dream once more. Initially my dreams found life in the local church. In the teaching of Jesus, I found encouragement to look at the world not as it is, but as it was intended to be. Jesus's teachings on the kingdom of God led me to dream of what it would look like when God's kingdom comes on earth. For a long time I kept my dreams to myself. I thought I was the only one questioning the status quo. I assumed the blow to my heart had sensitized me to the deeper questions of life.

What I discovered is that most people are secretly dreaming of a world different than the one that continually attempts to seduce us into complacency. I discovered many who through heartbreak and pain have found a reason to truly live. In the stories that follow, I hope you will hear

1

> *What I discovered is that most people are secretly dreaming of a world different than the one that continually attempts to seduce us into complacency.*

echoes of your own dreams and find the courage to seek out the intersection of your dreams and the world's needs. There is more to life than running faster and faster on the hamster wheel. It took death to awaken me to life. I hope that through my journey and the wisdom of guides I have met along the way, you too will find your way to the intersection where the needs of a hurting world meet the dreams and callings of God's people.

My journey toward this intersection took an interesting turn in late 2001, when the demise of Enron turned my life upside down. My husband had been working for the multinational energy company for five years. We had just completed the construction of our dream home and had wiped out our savings account in the process. Since more than half of our retirement funds were in the form of Enron stock, we were left with almost no financial resources. The aftermath of Enron caused the collapse and downsizing of numerous energy-related businesses in the Houston area, and despite five months of aggressive searching my husband was unable to find employment. I was working as a part-time staff member at a local church, making almost nothing. In order to survive, we uprooted our family and moved to Richmond, Virginia.

The decision to leave Houston was the most difficult decision my husband and I had made in our fourteen years of marriage. We are both native Texans and left our family behind. Moving to Virginia altered our lives dramatically and sent us in a direction we likely never would have taken in Houston.

In those months after the fall of Enron, my husband and I experienced firsthand the humiliation of not being able to provide for our family. Members of our extended family helped us pay our mortgage, and church friends gave gifts to our children at Christmas. While the generosity of others overwhelmed us, and we were immensely grateful, the whole experience taught us a great deal about humility. It is far easier to give than it is to receive. Something dies inside a person when they are forced to ask others for help.

My husband and I were among the lucky ones who escaped the crash of Enron with only a minor setback. We were young and able to start over. We had the support of a loving family and a strong network of friends. Others were not so lucky. We often think of homelessness as something only the poorest of the poor experience, but the reality is that millions of Americans are only one job loss, one illness, or one accident away from losing their homes.

When I arrived in Richmond, I did not come seeking to understand homelessness. All I wanted to do was to put those difficult days in Houston behind me and start over. I wanted to go back to the life my husband and I had had before the Enron disaster. I wanted to live a simple suburban life and raise my children, and forget about the losses we had incurred.

In Houston I had been on staff at a church we loved. We started our journey in Richmond by looking for a similarly dynamic and exciting church. Instead we found the rather somber church environment of the east coast. No matter where we went, we walked away feeling as if we did not belong. After more than a year of frustrating church encounters, I was asking myself, "What is church? What is it that I am searching for?"

I began reading everything I could find about the church and what was going on in faith communities across the country. We had left a purpose-driven, seeker-friendly church in Houston: the kind of church that sought to attract the unchurched through relevant teaching, a casual environment, and contemporary music. The church had grown rapidly and had a worship attendance of more than eight thousand at the time we left. Unfortunately while the seeker model was being replicated in a number of churches in Richmond, they all felt hollow and without substance. Looking back, I do not think it was the churches; I think somehow we had been changed by the Enron experience. The old ways of living our faith no longer held as much meaning as they had before. I can't really explain it except to say we felt like misfits. Though we had a physical home, we were spiritually homeless.

In my journey to discover what was missing from our church experience, I ran across a paper titled "Ten Paradigm Shifts toward Community Transformation," written by Eric Swanson of Leadership Network, which opened with these words: "All over the nation there is a quiet movement of the Spirit of God that is causing believers to reexamine how they 'do church.' Churches across the nation are throwing out old measures of success. It is no longer merely about size, seeker sensitivity, spiritual gifts, church health, nor the number of small groups. It's about making a significant and sustainable difference in the lives of people around us—in our communities and in our cities."[1]

That was it! I wanted to connect with a group of Christians who were making a difference in the community; a group that was not pouring all its energy into attracting and entertaining seekers, but one that was seeking to be a blessing to the community.

Swanson goes on to provide a roadmap to finding that place: "Community transformation begins at the intersection of the needs and dream of a community, the calling and capacities of the church and the mandates and desires of God for a community."[2]

These words opened up a new path to me. Rather than journey from one church to another expecting to find the right fit, I decided instead to find the intersection of the needs and dreams of my community, the calling and capacities of God's people, and the desires of God. I knew that at this intersection I would find a movement of the Holy Spirit and a community of faith with whom I longed to connect.

As I made my journey, God used the stories of some amazing men and women to guide me along the way. Some shaped my journey in passing and profound ways while others have become lifelong friends. The story I share with you is true, or as true as my memory allows. I have changed the names and in some cases minor details to protect the identity of some of my friends who may not want to be identified. Throughout the writing of this book, I was allowed the privilege of conducting in-depth interviews with some of these wise counselors, who helped me better understand the more challenging issues I faced. These interviews appear as they were presented to me, and I have made no effort to validate the information that was shared. In most cases, contributors' names are authentic. However, in rare instances the names of these contributors have been changed to protect their privacy. I am indebted to these men and women for their willingness to share their stories with us, and for the invaluable wisdom they impart.

1. Swanson, "Ten Paradigm Shifts."
2. Ibid.

My dream: To find the intersection of the needs and dreams of my community, the calling and capacities of people of faith, and the mandates and desires of God for the community.

2 Dreaming of a Different Kind of Family

Jesus had a new definition of family, rooted in the idea that we are adopted as orphans into the family of God and that this rebirth creates a new kinship that runs deeper than biology or geography or nationality.

—SHANE CLAIBORNE

Three miserable months after we moved to Richmond, a neighbor made the inadvertent mistake of asking me how I liked Richmond. "I hate it!" I blurted out. I suspect my honesty caught her off guard. Being the hospitable person she is, Karen asked me why. I proceeded to tell her how it had been difficult for me to make friends. She asked me what I had enjoyed doing back in Houston.

"I was a small group coordinator for my church. I coordinated small groups where Christians could get together to pray and study the Bible," I said.

"Why not start one here in Richmond?" she asked.

"That'd be one really lonely small group. I don't know anyone," I said.

Karen confessed that her Catholic upbringing had not emphasized the study of Scripture, but she said she'd love an opportunity to be part of such a group—and then offered to help me start one! The group, which we nicknamed the Yada Yadas, consisted of five Catholic ladies (friends of Karen's), one Presbyterian (one of my neighbors), and me (the confused nondenominational, Methodist-Baptist-Lutheran mutt).

The Yada Yadas had been meeting for about a year when I discovered the aforementioned paper by Swanson about community transformation and began my search for that intersection of the needs, dreams, and callings of our community. I decided to try an experiment. I gave the ladies large sheets of paper and colored markers and told them to draw pictures that would illustrate how they would complete the sentence, "If I could do anything for God and knew I would not fail, I would . . ." Some of my friends looked at me with blank stares as if to say, "Are you serious? You want us to draw?"

For about twenty minutes, these seven suburban soccer moms contemplated their God-given dreams. No one wanted to be first to reveal her fragile dreams, but I didn't let these ladies off the hook.

Aileen finally volunteered. Her drawing depicted suburban women embracing single mothers in the inner city. Aileen was the born dreamer of the group and had learned at a tender age to treasure life. Her picture came as no surprise to any of us. In the first few months of our group's existence, Aileen had shared that she had always dreamt of being a foster parent. For months the group encouraged her to share her dreams with her husband, but she had not been able to, afraid he'd reject the idea. So she wrote him an e-mail. Rick and Aileen's third child was conceived over the information superhighway. For months the Yada Yadas prayed that Aileen and Rick would get a foster child. Unfortunately their first experience in foster parenting was brief and painful: Aileen bonded with a beautiful premature baby boy who had been abandoned in the hospital, only for him to be returned to his biological family. After a season of grieving, Aileen and Rick renewed their commitment to being foster parents.

The day finally arrived for them to welcome Rhonny, a heroin-addicted newborn, into their home. Night after night as the poor, fragile child withdrew from the drugs, Aileen rocked the tormented babe and implored God to ease his pain. Even with the morphine and methadone treatments, he seemed to find no relief. As the intensity of his cries grew, so did Aileen's anger and frustration toward the child's biological mother, until one day she asked the group, with tears streaming down her face.

"Pray I stop hating her. How could anyone do this to their child? What kind of mother takes drugs when she is pregnant? I do not want to hate her. Please pray for me." It was the most heartfelt prayer I had ever heard.

As we all held hands and prayed for Aileen, we also prayed for the child's biological mother, whom Aileen would have to face the following week at the doctor's office. Inside, Aileen was being pulled apart. She had lost a brother to addiction and had always seen drug addiction as an illness and not a choice. However, as she held that innocent, tiny child in her arms, she did not know what to do with those feelings of anger that were stirred up inside her. They were mixed with emotions of grief for the brother she had lost, sympathy for this mother who was losing her child, and her deep love for this child who was suffering unjustly.

Aileen had only briefly seen the woman who had given birth to her foster son. The sighting happened at a court hearing a few days after the child's birth. Little Rhonny was still in the hospital where he would remain for five weeks. Aileen had been surprised that Via chose to appear in court that day; it was obvious she was still in active addiction. She was a dark-skinned black woman in her early thirties, with matted hair pulled up in two short, stubby ponytails that protruded from the top of her head. She wore blue jeans and sneakers, and her T-shirt was on inside out! She stared off into space, physically present but emotionally and mentally absent from the entire proceeding.

The first face-to-face meeting between Aileen and Via was to be at Rhonny's doctor's appointment. Aileen secretly hoped that Via would not show up. But when Via walked in the door, it was obvious something had changed. The glassy-eyed trance-like state Aileen had witnessed in the courtroom had been replaced with an enthusiastic, childlike spirit. Via eagerly shared that she was in treatment and was attending Narcotics Anonymous. She then said, "Mrs. Eilaney," which is what she called Aileen for the first year of their relationship, "I is going to make it this time, cuz God is going to help me." While inside, Aileen was dying of grief over the thought of losing Rhonny, something about this woman's hope-filled eyes and her faith in God's power began to soften Aileen's heart, and she found herself praying for Via.

At her next meeting with the child's social worker, Aileen shared that she would like to spend more time with Rhonny's biological mother, but the social worker urged her not to, saying it typically only made things more complicated. Against the professional's advice, Aileen began writing Via notes about how Rhonny was doing, then inviting her out to lunch, and finally talking by phone between visits. She soon realized that Via had been born into a vicious cycle of poverty, drugs, and poor education. It was obvious to Aileen that despite the poor choices Via had made during her pregnancy, she truly loved Rhonny. It also became clear that Rhonny, and the hope that one day she'd truly be able to be his mother, was giving Via the strength to overcome her addiction.

Something had happened to Via between that first court appearance and her first real visit with her son. Via had come alive and had found inside herself the strength to fight her illness. Rhonny was not the first child she had lost to addiction, but she wanted him to be the last. For the last twelve years she had been on a merry-go-round to try to overcome her cravings: Narcotics Anonymous (NA) and healing services, going cold turkey and to drug rehab centers. No matter how much she tried to break free, round and round she went. In those weeks of visiting Rhonny in the hospital and witnessing what the drugs were doing to his tiny body, she vowed to get off that ride once and for all.

Several weeks after Rhonny's birth, Via and her sister, Genell, who also suffered from heroin addiction, found themselves sitting outside the local Methadone clinic. Genell warned, "You know, if we do this and it don't work, the withdrawals are ten times worse than heroin."

"Yeah, I know," replied Via. "But, Nell, I just can't do it no more. I can't go back. I got to do it for Rhonny."

Together they committed to treatment. The cost was high at twelve dollars a day and $150 up front. They had to borrow the money from family members and had no idea how they were going to afford the treatment drugs on a daily basis since neither of them had jobs. The odds of them making it, even on Methadone, were very slim.

As Aileen's relationship with Via grew, she was surprised to find how alike they were. Both were from large families: Aileen was one of nine who

Over time, Aileen stopped looking at Via as an addict and started looking at her as an equal: a woman, a mother, a sister.

had grown up in an Irish-Catholic family, and Via was one of twelve who had grown up in the projects in Richmond; both had lost brothers to addiction, and both had endured painful childhood experiences. Over time, Aileen stopped looking at Via as an addict and started looking at her as an equal: a woman, a mother, a sister. Aileen shared with me that "through infant massage to help heal Rhonny, Via and I bonded and began to pray together, which helped us both to let go of the fear and to stop seeing each other as a threat. The intimate setting of this class allowed me time to understand that Via didn't 'do' this to Rhonny."

When Rhonny was almost one, the big court date arrived. Rhonny would be returning home. Aileen stood in front of the judge and shared that she felt Via was ready to be a parent, and assured the judge that no matter what the ruling was, she and her husband would continue to support Via in her parenting efforts. To celebrate the judge's decision to reinstate Via's parental rights, Aileen and her family took Via out to lunch. While Aileen had the utmost confidence in Via's ability to be a good mom, Via was nervous about being on her own. She pulled Aileen off to the side and said, "I want you and me to be Rhonny's mommies together." Over the next few weeks they worked out a schedule whereby Rhonny would spend time with both his mommies. This arrangement freed up Via to find full-time employment, and made the transition of coming back to his birth mother less stressful on Rhonny.

Aileen and Via's friendship continued to grow into a special bond that defies logic. During Via's one-year ceremony at her NA group, Aileen stood proudly beside Via as she accepted her hard-earned one-year chip. Aileen broke into tears when later that day Via gave the chip to her.

"Without you, Mrs. Eilaney, I do not think I would have made it this far." Aileen wears that chip around her neck at all times. It is her most prized possession.

In the spring of 2005, Rick, Aileen, and Via were told that they were making Virginia history, when the courts granted joint legal custody of Rhonny. According to social workers on this case, for the first time in Virginia and possibly in the United States, foster parents and a biological parent would share custody. Rhonny would now have both his families for the rest of his life.

More than three years after starting methadone treatment, Via paid her final twelve dollars to the Richmond Treatment Center. She had beaten the odds. It had been a long and difficult journey, but her newfound sister, Aileen, had been with her every step of the way. She had held a job for three years, and she had found an apartment she could afford.

In 2007, Aileen became severely ill with pancreatitis. Aileen and Rick now needed Via's help. They invited Via to move in with them, and both families now live under one roof. In the past four years, Aileen and Rick adopted two additional foster children. They are the most amazing family I know.

What prompted Aileen to reach out to Via? I believe it was her own pain. Aileen had lost a brother to liver failure as a result of his drug addiction two years earlier. She did not hate her brother for his illness, so how could she hate Via? She would have given anything to help her brother avoid his untimely end. Through her love of Via, she was able to demonstrate to our entire community the grace and love that we should all have for our hurting brothers and sisters, both biological and spiritual. Aileen will tell you that Via is just as much a sister to her as her eight biological siblings.

That evening back in 2003 when I asked Aileen to dream, she drew a picture of dozens of suburban women embracing urban single mothers. Imagine a world full of Aileens and Vias! What if every Rhonny had two mommies? Aileen challenged us all to see the world differently. She also allowed us all to be a part of this great big, beautiful family to which she had given life. In reality, Rhonny had eight mommies, Via, Aileen, the other five Yada Yadas, and me. One of the greatest honors I have ever received was being asked to be Rhonny's godmother. I cannot wait to see what God does through the life of this amazing little boy whose birth brought together an entire community.

As Aileen shared her vision of women like herself leaving the suburbs and entering the inner city of Richmond, I was struck by her confidence and by how much she had grown in the time I had known her. I will never forget the first small-group meeting Aileen attended. Before the group began, Aileen pulled me off to the side and whispered, "I have to tell you something. I have never read the Bible before." She looked like a scared little child who feared she would be called upon and humiliated in front of her friends. Then for the closing prayer, I made the mistake of asking all the ladies to stand in a circle and pray one by one. Aileen looked at me with a shocked expression and asked, "Out loud? I'm Catholic. We don't pray out loud!"

Now here she stood a year later, challenging the rest of us to trust in God. Somehow Via had affected Aileen's life as much as Aileen had affected hers. Watching Via struggle with addiction, poverty, lack of education, lack of employment, lack of transportation, lack of affordable housing, and on and on, had changed Aileen. Via had become a spiritual guide for Aileen. Via had refused to give up, always claiming that God would lead her to victory. Though Via only had an eighth-grade education, she devoted herself to reading Scripture. She attended her NA meetings daily and never missed church. Every biblical promise she discovered was like a rung on a ladder, leading her out of a pit of darkness, and Aileen on a journey of discovery into the power of faith.

> *Every biblical promise she discovered was like a rung on a ladder, leading her out of a pit of darkness, and Aileen on a journey of discovery into the power of faith.*

I will never forget sitting in Via's living room shortly after we had met. Aileen had told me that Via was eager to study the Bible, and I had gone to visit her to discuss starting a small group in the public-housing project near where she lived. As we sat in her tiny cinderblock living room, a roach scurried across the concrete floor. She nonchalantly smashed it with her shoe as she proceeded to tell me that she was the richest woman I knew. I asked her how she had become so rich, and she said, "'Cause I have learned what is important and what is not." To this day, Via is one of the wealthiest women I know. She is still making seven dollars an hour cleaning up the local ballpark, but she knows more joy and is full of more love than most of my neighbors making six-figure salaries.

Insights from Aileen

When Via asked me to help her parent Rhonny, I was not surprised. Via is an addict and always will be an addict. She needs to live her life one day at a time for survival, and without a strong family support system, statistically the system was setting her up for failure. One parenting class just wasn't enough for her to believe she could do this. She loved Rhonny enough to make sure that if for some reason she had a setback, he would be in a safe, happy environment where he could thrive.

I would be lying if I didn't admit to having had feelings of anger and resentment toward Via at first. After all, I was the one taking care of a very sick baby, and I fell in love with him in the process.

However, today Via and I are so much more than friends and co-parents: we are true sisters. Maybe not from the same gene pool, but we know that we are closer than most "real" sisters and have made a lifetime commitment to one another and our son.

Via is my hero, my sister, and my best friend. She is the strongest woman I know. She has beaten every statistic for recovery because she wanted to live and she didn't want to blow the chance to be a mommy to Rhonny. She is a constant source of positive energy for me. She always lives for the moment and rarely worries about the past or the inequality of life.

Co-parenting with Via has been one of the most fulfilling experiences of my life. If our story reaches out to one addict, one social worker, or one foster parent, and helps them see their relationship in a new light, then we have made a difference in the life of a child and in the system. While there have been many trials and tribulations along the way, I wouldn't change one single thing.

I pray more good people will consider foster parenting, knowing that they can build a friendship with the birth family. It may not be for everyone, but for many I think it could work if they just gave it a chance!

Insights from Via

When I was using, life was hard. I thought for sure I would die an addict. Of my twelve brothers and sisters, all but two are heroin addicts. I hated them growing up, and then I became just like them. My brother-in-law said that I was born to be an addict; it is just in my genes. When I started getting clean, it felt like I was leaving behind my family. I don't think they like me clean. I think they want me like I used to be, and it has been hard. I have had to walk away from my family in order to build a healthy home for Rhonny.

When Rhonny was in the hospital, all I felt was guilt: guilt for having hurt my baby, guilt that I had caused him pain. So I did not go very often to see him, but I never really thought they would take him from me. I thought he would come home with me.

Then I found out about the foster family, and that they was going to take my baby. All I knew was that some white woman was trying to take my baby. I had to get clean for Rhonny. That is why I went to the clinic. I had to fight for my baby. But people kept telling me that was not a strong enough reason. I had to do it for me. They also told me that I could not do it on my own; I needed a higher power. I never believed in God, so why would a God I did not believe in help me?

When I first started getting clean, I started reading the Bible, and everything started to look different. I never noticed the sky or the stars or the trees when I was using. I never liked that stuff, but when I started getting clean, I started to really love those things. I started to really love life, and I wanted others to find this freedom.

Everyone I knew was an addict, but when I got clean, it inspired others to get clean. I have more than twenty friends I used to hang with on the street who got clean after I did. They remembered what I was like, and I think they thought, "If Via can do it, I can do it." I think that is what God wants me to do, to help my sisters beat their addiction, and if we help just one woman, then it is all worth it.

I am an addict and I will always be an addict, but I do not think I will ever use again, I really do not think I will ever use again. I know God will help me through the difficult times in my life. My worst days clean are far better than my best days using 'cause I know God is going to help me—maybe not right away, maybe not in a day or a week, but I know at some point, God will help me.

She saw something in me I did not even see in myself. She helped me discover a life worth living, a life worth fighting for, a life I never dreamed I would have.

I want to thank Aileen. She is my dearest sister. After God and Rhonny, I love Aileen best. Aileen loved me when no one else saw the good in me. When others only saw an addict, she saw me as her sister. She saw something in me I did not even see in myself. She helped me discover a life worth living, a life worth fighting for, a life I never dreamed I would have. I love that lady!

Insights from Rick, Tim, and Katy

No one can do great things without a tremendous amount of support. Aileen's husband, Rick, and two children, Tim and Katy, are the unsung heroes of this story. They opened their home and their hearts to Rhonny, Via, Tommy, and Tia, who are all now members of the Owens family. Below are their reflections on this journey from your typical American family to this new and improved family unit.

Reflections from Aileen's Husband, Rick

I think in the beginning, Aileen and I lumped Via into a stereotype. We had been jaded by all the negative images of addicted women having babies in the inner city, and I think at some level we both judged her. The biggest reason why I think the relationship between Via and Aileen formed was because of Via's willingness to open up and to trust Aileen. There never was an adversarial relationship with Via. I never felt like she looked at us as the enemy. Once that initial trust was built, we were able to work more as partners.

I had not really spent a lot of time with Via prior to our decision to co-parent, but I had witnessed her commitment to being a parent to Rhonny through her actions. I saw how she had overcome every obstacle; she got a job, stayed clean, found an apartment. I also watch her reinforce our attempts to parent Rhonny. She never tried to undo our parenting or undermine us. After being in this kind of complementary relationship for a while, co-parenting was just a formal extension of what we were already doing. The transition to actually having Via live in our home has been a much easier adjustment than I thought it would be. For me, the most significant thing was to make sure that Via absolutely wanted this. I think it has worked well because we are all on the same page. There is no hidden agenda. Via is not looking to gain anything from us, and we are not trying to take advantage of her. So far, we all love the arrangement.

The biggest thing that I have learned from Via is not to be quick to rush to judgment. Not everyone who lives in the inner city is a bad person, and many are not there by their own choice. It is really hard to get an appreciation for life in the inner city living out here in the suburbs where we live. We watch the news or read the paper, and all we see is the negative stuff. I think it is important that people realize that for some people, all it takes is a trigger to motivate them to make a change, and a positive support system to encourage them along the way.

Reflections from Aileen's son Tim—age 16

When I first heard that my mom and dad were going to be foster parents, my first thought was "Wow, this is going to be cool." I was only ten, and I did not really get the responsibility part. When I was around thirteen, I began to realize what a significant role we were playing in helping these kids and their families. Being the eldest in a home with three foster children is a lot of work. However, I would rather have a challenging experience where I learn more and have responsibility, because it makes me a better person than a life that is just like everyone else's . . . just going along and not facing challenges until I am older.

If we did not have Rhonny, Thomas, and Tia in our lives, life would be boring. I also love the relationship that we have with Via. I think it is really important that Rhonny have a relationship with his biological mother. I love having Via in the house. She gives me my own space, and she helps out tremendously with the kids and all the responsibilities in the house. Our house is busy and always full of activity, but I love it.

Reflections from Aileen's daughter, Katy—age 14

When my mom and dad first shared that we were going to be foster parents, I did not realize that we would have them forever. I thought it was kind of like babysitting overnight. When the first baby had to be returned to the biological parents, I wanted to stop because it was so hard letting go. However, the hardest part was when Mom and Dad went to court with Via, and Mom told us that Via had regained custody of Rhonny. I thought we would never see him again. I was not allowed to go to the court, and that was the longest five hours of my life.

I was so happy when they decided to co-parent. I was thrilled to have Rhonny in my life, and I was also happy that we would get to know Via more. It has been amazing having Via in the house. Sometimes she is more like one of the kids than an adult. She is more of a friend to me than a parental figure. In the morning she is the first person I see, and when I go to bed at night, she is the last person I talk to. She is like a big sister to me.

Being a foster sister has changed my perspective on a lot of things, especially as it relates to race. I honestly do not even notice racial difference. I have had some teachers who have said "You have 'black' kids in your family?" It blows my mind that some people simply focus on race and not on the relationships we have. What is funny is that I have actually heard more comments from black individuals who seem puzzled that a "white" family is taking in "black" kids. It seems to be that some black people assume that all white people do not like black people. It confuses me, because honestly we are all the same. I just don't get it.

Aileen's dream: To be liaison between the different members of the foster-care team (biological families, social workers, and foster parents).

Via's dream: To help other women who have lost their children due to addiction.

3 The Yada Yadas' Dream

Be the change you want to see in the world.
—MOHANDAS GANDHI

How do you follow a dream like Aileen's? No one in that group of women thought their dream as worthy as hers. However, Karen hesitantly held up her picture. The sensible one in the group, Karen always kept us on task, remembering to bring the snacks, and reminding us to schedule our next meeting. She has an incredible gift of hospitality. When you are in her presence, you feel loved and accepted and welcome.

While dreaming was not something that came naturally to Karen, when given the time and the space, she could dream. Her dream was one of practicality. She held up a picture with trucks on it and explained, "Our neighborhood has so much excess. We have far more stuff than we need. If I could do anything, I would take the excess of the suburbs and carry it into the city and give it away to people in need." That night in 2003, none of us had a clue that by 2007 we would have given away the equivalent of over three hundred households of furniture. But that story will have to wait. Karen was just dreaming that night. She had no plans of actually living the dream, and neither did the rest of us. This was just pie in the sky . . . or so we thought.

Next came Colleen, with her dream of going to Africa and working with orphaned children. Then Eileen, with hers of working with emotionally disturbed children. MaryJo dreamed of sharing her musical talents with underprivileged children. Cynthia dreamed of becoming a teacher in the inner city.

As one by one each of these women shared her dream, we all felt a growing sense of God's presence in the room. All the dreams seemed to complement one another, and all of them were focused on the needs of others, in particular on the poor. No one dreamt of winning the lottery or building a bigger house or going on some extravagant vacation. Everyone dreamt of making a difference in the world.

It was finally my turn. My picture was of a van, a mobile-ministry van. My dream was to gather up all the dreamers and help them see their dreams come true. My thought at the time was to build missional small groups across the city that would help people discover their callings and to support one another in seeking to be faithful to that call. I had no idea how or whether this dream would ever become a reality. But in time, that one small group of seven suburban women grew into Quest, a women's ministry with seven small groups and over seventy women, whose mission is "to empower women to live their God-given dreams by nurturing their love of God, self, and others."

Quest provided women an opportunity to develop authentic relationships through which they could truly share their lives, thoughts, and dreams with one another. This kind of intimate community is rare. However, there is something "magical" or divinely powerful about such a group, especially when that group invites God to do miraculous things in and through it.

Once our initial small group had begun, over the next two years, I met dozens of women like the Yada Yadas: women who had been blessed with great talents and abilities, and who desired to do more with their lives than simply to build their own human kingdoms, but instead to invest themselves in the lives of others.

Some of the Yada Yada women already volunteered at schools, others at their local churches; but few had been able to find opportunities to fully live their dreams. I was surrounded by an army of mighty warriors who had somehow gotten lost and could no longer see the enemy. Instead of fighting for justice, we had been told to shop, take care of our own families' needs, and let others address the needs of the world.

The church had told us that our role in doing "outreach" was to invite friends to come to worship, but no one had ever challenged us to go beyond the walls of the church or the comfort of our own com-

> *No one had ever challenged us to go beyond the walls of the church or the comfort of our own community.*

munity. No one had ever suggested that God's kingdom exists in places without steeples and pulpits. Bombarded with messages about the dangers of the city, we were consumed by fear of the strangers on the other side. Most of us had elected to live in this distant suburb of Richmond to escape the crime of the city, so the thought of intentionally going back was like asking the Israelites who had made it to the Promised Land to return to Egypt.

Despite dozens of workshops on discerning one's call and the dozens of God-inspired pictures drawn through the years, few have been willing to respond to the call to care for the poor. For some it is simply not the season; but for most it is fear that paralyzes, and the whisperings of the world that seduce them to take up a different cross: the cross of economic gain and self-interest.

As God called me into the inner city to work with Via and her friends, I felt the disconnect growing between the inner-city culture and the suburban culture where I lived. As my frustration increased with the complacency I found all around me, I realized that Quest was the launching pad for something else: something none of us could have foreseen.

In 2003 *New York Times*–bestselling author Bruce Wilkinson wrote a wonderful little book titled *The Dream Giver*. It is a parable about a Nobody named Ordinary, from a town called Familiar. One day Ordinary receives a message from the Dream Giver. "Nobody was made to be a Somebody and destined to achieve Great Things."[1] The story chronicles all the trials Ordinary endures as he journeys from the Comfort Zone of Familiar toward his Big Dream. As he attempts to cross the boarder of Familiar, Ordinary hits the invisible Wall of Fear. Ordinary has to make a choice: "He could either keep his comfort or his Dream."[2] Ordinary pushes through the wall of fear, only to come face to face with Border Bullies, who he thought were his friends. They try to convince him to turn back, and they question the wisdom of his

1. Wilkinson, *The Dream Giver*, 14.
2. Ibid., 25.

choice. Refusing to turn back, Ordinary faces the Giant of Unbelief and finally arrives at the city gates of Anybody. "The needs of the Anybodies were great, and their hopes were few . . . The Big Needs of the Anybodies matched perfectly the Big Dream in his heart, and it was time to do his dream . . . He saw the need nearest him and tried to meet it."[3] For a long while, Ordinary lives out his dream in the city of Anybody until one day he hears the Dream Giver calling him to go further, and he realizes he is ready for the dream to grow into a new and bigger Dream.

We all feel like Nobodies—too ordinary to achieve great things. We feel as if the world and its problems are far too big for us to have any kind of beneficial impact on it. So we settle for running on the hamster wheel, chasing after "stuff" and "pleasure," ignoring our dreams and settling for the latest and greatest goody this world has to offer. Then along comes someone like Aileen or Via: someone so unselfish, so willing to sacrifice for others, that all our tireless spinning and toiling seem utterly pointless.

I have not been able to duplicate the chemistry of the Yada Yada group over the years. That group was a gift from God for a season when all seven of us needed to be inspired to dream. We were together to comfort Cynthia when her mother died and to care for Colleen as she defeated breast cancer, and it was this group who encouraged me to follow my dream of going to seminary and starting a ministry of building bridges between communities of prosperity and poverty. They were the safe little nest I needed, for a while. But as God tends to do to us, eventually I was pushed out of my place of comfort so my dreams could grow wings and fly.

During my years leading Quest Women's Ministry, I discovered the first key element in Swanson's roadmap to community transformation: I discovered the dreams of God's people.

A few brave souls made the journey and carried all those dreams into the city to discover where they intersected with the community's needs. In addition to Aileen, Karen was one of those faithful people willing to continue the journey even when it meant personal sacrifice. She journeyed with me from our first encounter at the bus stop through countless hours with the Yada Yadas, became our first board President, and eventually lived her dream by becoming the first paid director of

3. Ibid., 62.

Virginia's only furniture bank. Karen embodies what it means to practice Christian hospitality toward the stranger.

Insights from Karen O'Brien

Welcoming new people at the bus stop is just something I do. That is actually how I first met Aileen. I love meeting new people, especially people who have different life experiences than I have. I remember visiting with Wendy on my back porch and listening to her talk about her life experiences and her faith.

I grew up in Rochester, New York, and while my family was very involved in the Catholic Church, we did not engage in spiritual conversations outside Sunday worship. I wanted to be around people like Wendy; she was so open and comfortable sharing her faith, and I knew that helping her start a small group would stretch me.

That night when Wendy asked us to draw our dreams, it was a struggle. Dreaming is not something I really allow myself time to do. However, as we sat there I just realized how blessed we are. We all have far more than we need. I spend a lot of time managing stuff, and it takes away from other, more important things. In the suburban community where I live, there is such abundance, and I do not like to see things go to waste.

I think it goes back to an experience I had back when I was eight or nine years old. I was in church, and I read a prayer that said that everything is God's, and that we are just the caretakers of God's things; none of it is ours. That realization changed me. My husband and I have always given things away and shared what we have with others. It is just kind of who we are. It has always worked so that when we share with others, we somehow always have what we need when we need it. Before that night I had never really thought about doing this kind of thing in an organized way.

I think there is a need for opportunities to share our things with those in need, not only to meet the needs of the recipient, but also to meet the needs of the giver. Jesus said we are to clothe the naked and feed the hungry. While I admire Aileen and others like her who are able to befriend those in need, not everyone is able or would feel comfortable going into the inner city. Giving material goods provides an opportunity for everyone to get involved and can sometimes be the bridge to building relationships.

Karen's Dream: To help expand into other communities the ministries she has helped start in Richmond.

---

4 Dreams of a Stranger

I believe that the gospel is a call to imitate a Jesus who reaches out to the undeserving. That, to me, is what grace is all about.

—TONY CAMPOLO

Encouraged by the Yada Yadas to follow my dreams, I entered seminary. I was leaving a world where I fit in, a world of thirty-something women with children and husbands and minivans, and I was entering a world of twenty-somethings with two-door cars, no child seats, and freedom. I felt like a misfit that first semester, entering with only a handful of other students, none of whom were minivan-driving moms from the suburbs. I felt awkward and seemed to trip over my own feet and bump into people at every turn. I felt like a high-school freshman all over again, except this time I had been held back fifteen years!

My spring semester was a lonely one, but I loved my classes. It was in Christian Ethics that first semester that I first heard the term "Christian hospitality." Before reading Christine Pohl's book *Making Room: Recovering Hospitality as a Christian Tradition*, I thought hospitality was about hosting parties and entertaining friends and neighbors. Pohl introduced me to a rebellious countercultural side of hospitality: the side of hospitality that sought to embody Jesus's words in Matthew 25:30 that "what you did for one of the least of these, you did for me." Pohl writes, "Although we often think of Hospitality as a tame and pleasant practice, Christian hospitality has always had a subversive, countercultural dimension. 'Hospitality is resistance' . . . Especially when the larger society disregards or dishonors certain persons, small acts of respect and

24

welcome are potent far beyond themselves. They point to a different system of valuing and an alternate model of relationships."[1]

An invitation arrived in my inbox one day that would allow me to practice this ancient Christian tradition of hospitality; it was an invitation to join a team from Prison Fellowship ministering in the Goochland Correctional Facility. In Matthew's gospel, Jesus reminds us that when we visit those in prison, we are visiting him. I decided to give it a try. Yet when the time came, I did not want to go. I kept asking myself, "Why am I doing this?" My resistance masked an underlying fear. Once I arrived at the prison, it took me twenty minutes to summon the courage to climb out of my car.

I watched the inmates walk down the steps into the basement where our Bible study was to be held. My heart was pounding, and my mind was racing: "They are going to hate me . . . What can I possibly say to these women? . . . I will never be able to relate to their world . . . They will not want to hear from someone like me . . . I have nothing to offer them."

Twenty inmates stood talking in the far corner of the basement. As I entered the room, a large, African American woman named Frances made a beeline for me. A huge, toothless grin adorned her face, and her arms were spread wide, ready to embrace me. I panicked: the Prison Fellowship training class had insisted that under no circumstances were we to hug the prisoners. As I looked to the guard to pull her gun and stop this violation, the enormous woman wrapped her arms around me and lifted me six inches off the ground. I could not help but hug her back. She lowered me to the ground and said with a thick southern accent, "Welcome, Sister Wendy!"

Those three words changed everything. In an instant, they transformed me from a stranger to a sister. I was family, one of them, welcome in this foreign land. I had expected to extend hospitality and instead became its recipient. All my fear, all my insecurities, all the barriers that I had assumed would separate me from Frances were crushed in that em-

> *In an instant, they transformed me from a stranger to a sister. I was family, one of them, welcome in this foreign land.*

1. Pohl, *Making Room*, 61.

brace and lay shattered on the floor. In the basement of the Goochland Correctional facility, I had found a sister in Christ.

Frances introduced me to Abigail, a frail Caucasian woman who joined my small group during a breakout session. Apart from the tattoos on her hands, she would have fit easily into my suburban neighborhood. She was attractive, well educated, and had been a nurse. An addiction to prescription drugs led to abuse of street drugs, which had led to her incarceration. She shared how she had started attending church and reading the Bible in prison. She was eager to learn more about the Christian faith and inquired at length about what I was learning in seminary.

Abigail was being released in a few weeks and asked me to pray for her.

"Where are you going?" I inquired.

"Chesterfield," she said. "

Chesterfield! I live in Chesterfield," I responded. "Do you have a church home?"

"No, I never really went to church on the outside," she confessed. I shared with her that we belong to a church in the area and told her she should come to church with me. She paused, pulled her sleeves down over her tattooed hands and sheepishly said, "You seem like a really nice lady, but you know I would never fit in at your church."

I was speechless. I wanted to argue with her and say, "Yes you will. We have a lot of ex-felons in our church." But that would have been a lie. My church, like most suburban mainline-denominational churches, was made up of people who were a lot like me: white, suburban professionals with 2.3 kids, a minivan, and a six-figure income. We all looked alike: from our perfect homes to our well-manicured yards and on down to our groomed and pedigreed pets. We spent our spare time on a ballfield rooting for our children's sports teams or in the mall shopping for our already well-stocked homes. While I am sure members of my church would have greeted her warmly, she would never fit in.

Driving home that day, I wrestled with many things: Why did I feel so welcome in the basement of a prison surrounded by convicted felons? Why would my new friend Abigail never feel welcome with the one group whose very mission was to welcome people with a love and acceptance that surpasses understanding? Something was terribly wrong with this picture. My heart grieved, and I prayed, "Lord, let me meet an Abigail on the outside so that I can extend Christian hospitality to her as warmly as I have received it in the basement of the Goochland Correctional Facility."

This prayer should have come with a warning: Be careful what you pray for; sometimes you get more than you bargain for!

Frances passed away before I had a chance to tell her what a powerful effect that embrace had had on me. Years later I met Phyllis who reminded me of Frances. Like Frances, Phyllis was a large, African American woman who knows how to deliver powerful hugs. Like Frances, Phyllis spent many years in prison, and like Frances, she allowed God to transform her into an agent of peace and unity. This is her story.

Insights from Phyllis

At the age of eighteen, I got involved in drugs and crime. I was the black sheep of the family: the blackest of the black sheep. No one in my family had ever been to jail. Everyone looked at me in disbelief and constantly asked me, "What is wrong with you?"

I spent close to ten years of my life incarcerated, going in and out of jail over a twenty-year period. It took many trips through the system before I decided I did not want to be there anymore. I liked the game, I liked to hustle, and there was a kind of thrill to being sent to the penitentiary. I may be kind of odd in this respect, but I was the same person on the inside as I was on the outside, and I did pretty much the same things: dealing and using drugs. So, I really was not motivated to stay out of jail; the consequences were just a part of the game. I would get excited anticipating how I was going to do my time, how much I was going to hustle, who I was going to hook up with. All prison did was teach me how to be a better criminal—how to steal better, how to conceal my dope better. There was no rehabilitation. It's a school, we were all teachers, and I learned a lot. I used to go to the Bible studies and spiritual sessions to get out of my cell, see my girl-friends, and hustle drugs. I had a very sick mind during these times.

This last time was different; I was different. When I was in darkness, I could not see what crack and stealing were doing to me, or how my relationships were being destroyed. In the beginning it had been exciting; now, I was almost forty years old, and the excitement was gone. After years of slow decay, there was simply nothing worth living for. While I was caught up in that darkness, I honestly wanted to die. I wanted to die because I was just so disgusted with myself and everything I had done. I had jumped out of the airplane 999 thousand times, and nothing had ever changed. Every time I jumped, I went down harder than the time before.

One night I hit rock bottom. I lay on the floor trying to find the courage to kill myself. Thankfully, I was too much of a coward. After that experience, I realized I did not want to live that way anymore. Once I was ready, God put people in my life to help me. My mother was the most important person. I missed my mother tremendously when I was out there using. When I was at the bottom, it was my mother's voice I heard calling out to me in the wilderness, leading me out of darkness. It is amazing to me how strong my mother is. She suffered all those afflictions I caused her and still loved me. She would say, "She is mine, whether she is in jail, out of jail, on crack or not on crack. She is mine. I am the one that birthed her and I believe that one day she is going to bring me joy, because she is mine."

My near-death experience happened right before I was sentenced this last time. I entered prison finally ready to receive the spiritual messages I had always rejected. During this time, I met my pastor. She got my attention because she always had the coolest shoes, but it was her compassion that drew me to her; she really cared about what we had to say. I also met Mrs. Sarah, who became my mentor and eventually invited me to be her partner in ministry. I now help her run a reentry home for women ex-offenders.

There were also white people from the suburbs who came into the prison to minister—people who had no idea why God called them to prison. I saw many of them enter the prison and jump in fear when the door slammed behind them, scared half to death. I think most of that fear is because they were not sure what to expect, and their expectations have been set by what is shown on TV.

It was during this time that I had a transforming of my mind as it relates to white people. I used to hate white people. I grew up listening to people talk about white people and blaming white people for much of the suffering in my community, so I just hated them even though they had never done anything to me directly. I experienced a few little racial things growing up, and I thought to myself, "What my grandma said about white people is true!" That resentment just grew and grew over the years.

Then this last time I got locked up, my bunkmate was a white girl! I had to find a way to get over this resentment, to deal with that negative attitude about white people. As God would have it, the people who were coming and leading the spiritual sessions were a group from a predominately white congregation. My first experience with a white preacher was seeing Joyce Meyer on TV in jail, waiting to go to the penitentiary. As I watched her, she always seemed to be talking about what I was going through. She was instrumental in my life. I even wrote her a letter telling her how important she was in my life. When I wrote her that letter, it was a way of releasing some of my resentment toward white people.

However, it was the volunteers from that white church that really helped me find release from my prejudice once and for all. One day I was just sitting at church and everything was great. Then it was testimonial time, and I stood up and I said, "I have something to confess; I am challenged by the fact that I just don't like white people. I want you all to pray for me." Immediately they stopped everything and they showed me that they loved me. They all embraced me. One even kissed me on the lips: now that was a trip! Everyone was hugging me and smiling at me. It was an awesome experience that has impacted my life in so many ways.

Being in that Christian community in prison gave me confidence; it gave me a sense of self-worth. I began to believe that I can do this, I can live in a new way. I had leadership gifts, and that community helped me to use those gifts for others. I realized that everything is not about Phyllis anymore. I real-

> *Being in that Christian community in prison gave me confidence; it gave me a sense of self-worth. I began to believe that I can do this, I can live in a new way.*

ized that everyone has hurts, everyone is going through things, and if we can just stop being so selfish and start to give, then we receive the true blessing—not in a material sense, but in a spiritual sense.

I am the prodigal son who has returned home, and I am willing to be a servant in my father's home. I am OK with being a servant. I used to think about the big house and the fancy car. I grew up thinking that was what my life should look like. When I was hustling, I never lacked the material things. Now that I am living for others, I do not have the material wealth, and it took me some time to let go of those dreams of material possessions. I no longer want more stuff. I want more love, I want more joy, I want more peace. Those are the riches I seek.

I now go back into the prison system and speak to the prisoners. I have to go back. It's like going on a terrible ride at the fair and then seeing other people standing in line for that same bad ride. They are not aware of the terrible experience you had, and when you get off the ride you say, "That was scary!" and you go around telling everyone about your bad experience, hoping they will decide to get out of that line and avoid that ride. We all want to reduce the suffering of others if we can. That's why I go back.

Phyllis's dream: To speak a message of hope to a multitude of hurting outcasts: those who are in hiding in the crack houses, in the shelters, and in the prisons because no one remembers them.

---

5 Dreaming of Work

The rich man [in Luke 16] did not abuse Lazarus, didn't beat him or mistreat him; he simply ignored him, passing by him, day after day, with indifference . . . The rich man went to hell because of his appalling apathy and failure to act in the face of gross disparity between his wealth and Lazarus's poverty.

—RICHARD STEARNS

In seminary I was required to serve as a volunteer chaplain in an adult home: the kind of place that provides shelter to elderly and mentally challenged individuals who lack the resources or capacity to live on their own.

I arrived at the adult home, expecting to be greeted by the manager who, I had been told, would introduce me to the residents. Instead, she said, "Fine. Just talk to whomever you want," and returned to her paperwork. I wandered up and down the halls peeking into rooms, hoping to find a friendly face. The three-story brick building housed over one hundred residents, three to a room. The rooms were small and sparsely furnished with metal frame twin beds and one dresser. I roamed those halls in search of an opportunity to provide "pastoral care." I was not exactly sure what that was, but I had to write a paper about my encounter and could not leave until I had something to write about. Eventually, I found four residents playing cards. They would become four of my greatest teachers.

Opal greeted me first: "Hi, sweetie, you look lost."

"I am the new chaplain from the seminary," I replied tentatively.

The gentleman sitting across from her quickly lifted his head to reveal his rosy cheeks and nose when he heard I was a minister. He looked like Santa Claus with a scraggly white beard. Mr. Peterson introduced himself and invited me to sit next to him. "So, you're a preacher?" he asked. I was not sure how to respond. The title did not feel natural to me yet, but it turns out that Mr. Peterson was quite the theologian. He was not ordained, but in the thirty years he had driven a taxi, he learned a lot about people, and his wisdom lent great insight to our theological discussions over the next two years.

Mr. Peterson had worked hard his entire life, but when his wife was diagnosed with cancer, he exhausted the family's resources caring for her. After her death, his health deteriorated, and he found himself penniless and homeless. He did not want to be a burden to his daughter, so he ended up in the adult home. Despite the loneliness I know he felt, he had created a home here with his newfound friends.

The third cardplayer was twenty-nine-year-old William, who was quite absorbed pushing his Matchbox cars back and forth on the table, sometimes going over his cards, sometimes around them. I said hello, but he only averted his eyes and silently played with his cars. His hair was a wild, unkempt Afro and his eyes protruded from their sockets. He would later inform me that his mother had dropped him as a child, and that was why he was "not normal." I learned from other residents that his mother had abandoned him the year before. For three years, William carried a tattered letter his mother had sent him a few months after he had arrived. That letter promised to retrieve him one day: a promise never fulfilled.

The fourth member at the table that day was Mrs. Janie. Mrs. Janie thinks she's eighty-two. She doesn't really know; having been born at home, she didn't have a birth certificate. Neither Janie nor Opal had ever married. They had no family and spent their days watching soap operas and playing cards. Opal was also a mean crossword-puzzler with a smart mind and a keen wit.

While I enjoyed the company of my new friends, I despised visiting the home. It was the most depressing place I have ever been. The residents just sat and stared at the television, hour after hour. The air was stale, and the furnishings tattered and worn. The walls were colorless, bland with nothing to remind the residents of the beauty of the outside world. Few had visitors, and most spent the holidays alone.

My new friends, however, found joy and pleasure in the simplest things. One spring day, I took my six-year-old daughter with me to visit Mrs. Janie. My daughter loved to visit Mrs. Janie but sensed the oppression that loomed there and asked if we could all go for a walk. Mrs. Janie had not been outside in months. I watched her face light up at the sight of a magnolia tree in bloom. Her eyes sparkled as she gazed at a low-lying blossom. She then asked if she could have it. I snapped the twig and handed it to her. She inhaled the sweet fragrance of the flower. In the confines of that dank and foul place, Mrs. Janie's joints kept her from moving about much. But here in the open fresh air, her legs were young again. We walked for what seemed like miles, and marveling at every tree and flower Mrs. Janie outpaced both my young daughter and me. Sunshine, green grass, flowers, fresh air, freedom: these were all gifts—gifts I had never appreciated in my frenzied existence, gifts that Mrs. Janie unwrapped for me.

Sunshine, green grass, flowers, fresh air, freedom: these were all gifts—gifts I had never appreciated in my frenzied existence, gifts that Mrs. Janie unwrapped for me.

The world had looked at my impoverished, old, mentally and physically challenged friends and had judged them disposable. Society had shoved them to the edge of existence, tucked them out of sight, and forgotten them. Many had sunk into despair, just waiting for death to deliver them from what felt like a hellish existence. However, my tattered band of four unlikely friends represented the resistance; they were the remnant that refused to succumb to their circumstances and defied the prevailing forces that urged them to quietly accept their meager existence.

While Mr. Peterson was Caucasian, most of the residents were African American. But he was the ringleader of the gang of cardplaying radicals. He laughed at Opal's jokes and told her how beautiful she was. He challenged William, saying, "You are a young man; you can do great things with your life."

Over time, William emerged from his shell and began to trust me. One day Mr. Peterson instructed me to go look at William's bed. Standing over William's bed, I asked why we were looking at the bed, to which Mr. Peterson replied with a little wink, "Because William is the best bed maker in the house, don't you think so?" William blushed and looked at his feet. Standing over the neatly made bed, I asked William, "Do you like to make beds?" He shyly answered yes. Mr. Peterson told me that William made the beds of many of the other members of the house. I could not imagine anyone enjoying the chore of bed making, but William clearly did.

William was trying to save his money. He had dreams of getting on a bus and finding his family. He spent hours panhandling on the street corner, hoping to scrape together enough money for a few more match-box cars and an escape ticket. While the thought of William wandering aimlessly in some city with no one to care for him distressed me, I hoped that if he were able to build a better life here in Richmond, he would not want to run away. Surely someone out there had beds that William could make. I did a little research and learned there was a program for adults with developmental disabilities that would assist them in acquiring jobs. Maybe William could get a job in a hotel or a nursing home making beds.

"William, would you be interested in going through a program that would help you find a job?" I asked.

His eyes lit up, and he nodded his head up and down and smiled, saying, "Yes! Yes! Yes!"

So I met with the director of the rehabilitation program and she agreed to interview William. Since I was neither family nor legal guardian, I was not able to enroll him in the program. A letter was sent to William at the home with an application.

William never received the application. When he asked the adult-home manager, she told him he could not attend since his doctor's orders were that he could not leave the home. Yet I had seen William leave the building on several occasions to beg for money on the street corner. What little hope I had inspired in William vanished, and he again withdrew. I was just like everyone else in his life, making promises that I could not fulfill.

His doctor prescribed heavy doses of medications that left William virtually comatose. Within a few weeks, William was hospitalized for depression. I felt terrible. I never dreamt that bringing hope could lead to such a disastrous outcome. I attempted to speak to the manager about William and was told that my job was to make people feel better, to pray with them, but that I was not to get involved in their lives. William was never the same again. I saw him occasionally over the years, standing on the street corner panhandling. All he wanted to do was make beds. All he wanted was a little dignity. All we gave him were drugs and hopelessness. In our attempt to "protect" him, we sedated him and hoped he would simply fade into the wallpaper. There had to be a better way!

I was devastated. My pastoral-care professor offered little comfort. He had warned me that I was getting too close to the residents and needed better boundaries, or I would burn out. I dismissed his warnings and believed if I tried to live as Christ, all would work out. I had been unprepared for this outcome. Over and over again, I returned to the words of Matthew 25:40 "Truly I tell you just as you did it to one of the least of these who are members of my family, you did it to me" and asked myself, where was Christ in this encounter with William? The easy answers that my Christian faith had taught me up to this point did not satisfy. Something much larger than personal sin was at work here. It would not matter how much William prayed, it would not matter how many hours he spent in church, it would not matter how many biblical passages he could recite: the outcome would be the same. The system had already concluded that William should spend his days staring at soap operas and playing with matchbox cars. My lame attempts at freeing him from this system only caused him injury. This was my first conscious encounter with systemic evil.

After this encounter with William, I stopped visiting my friends at the adult home. Initially I refrained from visiting because I lacked answers, and as time slipped by, it was guilt that kept me away. Like everyone else, I abandoned them. The brokenness was too great and the needs too overwhelming for me to make a difference. If Jesus was in that place, he had long ago been crucified, and all attempts at resurrecting hope seemed doomed to fail. Like most well-meaning Christians, I learned to look past William on the corner of that intersection. I tried to pretend Opal, Janie, and Mr. Peterson would be fine without me. Instead of healthy boundaries, I opted for thick walls to protect me. Perhaps I was not cut out for urban ministry after all, I thought.

One of the questions I asked when I began working in the adult home was, where are the families of those who are living in these homes? Several years later, I met Kathy and Bob Jones, parents of John, a young man who suffered from mental illness. The Joneses live in my affluent neighborhood and are two of the most loving, caring individuals I have ever met. About the time I was getting to know William, their son was in a similar group home just down the street. This is their story.

Insights from Bob and Kathy

We adopted John when he was fourteen months old. John was a very good little boy; loving and obedient. However, as time went on, things deteriorated. By the time he was seven or eight, we realized we needed help with him. He would be very disruptive, always testing us. We had two other younger adopted children. If we were all together as a family enjoying an evening at home, John would find a way to disrupt the peace. We began going to counselors to try to get help, but they only focused on parenting skills. The teenage diagnosis of "inappropriate adolescent social development" prevented us from recognizing the seriousness of his mental illness. It was not until he was in his early twenties that he was diagnosed as suffering from schizophrenia.

When John was fifteen, things got out of control. He was totally unpredictable. Situations that we thought might trigger a negative response in him did not, whereas what to us seemed trivial issues brought forth his violent side. For example, I was on the phone one day. He came downstairs and asked me to take him someplace. I told him when I got off the phone I would take him. He turned around and went upstairs, grabbed the stereo that we had gotten him for Christmas, took it out into the driveway, and chopped it up with an ax as a way of punishing me. He was very disturbed.

When he was sixteen he quit school and began getting into trouble with the law, breaking into homes and doing other similar acts. The hardest part of all the things we went through with John was his violent behavior. We were scared to death of him. The professionals would ask us, "Are you afraid of him? Do you believe him when he says he is going to kill you?" We would say yes. And they would simply say, "Good. You should be afraid."

When we called the police because he was threatening us or being violent, they would tell us there was nothing they could do until he actually seriously hurt someone. This was *very* frustrating.

We did not realize it at the time, but John was abusing his younger siblings. The kids hid much of the abuse from us because John threatened to kill us if they told. I will never forget the first time I saw him attack one of the other children. They were eating dinner and all of a sudden, John jumped up, grabbed his little brother by his shirt and slammed him up against the wall for absolutely no reason. That is when we agreed we could no longer have him in the house.

We had several counseling sessions focusing on "tough love" before we could require that John do for himself. It was on John's eighteenth birthday that we moved him out. We rented him an apartment, furnished it, loaned him a car, and agreed to pay his rent for three months to give him time to find a job. At the end of three months, he claimed he could not find a job. The day before he was to be evicted from the apartment, he took all the furniture outside and chopped it up as a way of punishing us for not paying his rent.

He called the house at 3:00 a.m. that first night on the streets and said he was cold and hungry and had no place to go. It was the hardest thing in the world to do, but we had to tell him that we could not help him. Then miraculously the next day he got a job. He actually held one job for three years. But then that ended suddenly. The psychiatrist explained to us that it is common for people with schizophrenia to self-sabotage; nothing good ever lasted long for John. If things were going well, he made sure they would not stay that way.

During his late teens and early twenties, he was in and out of mental hospitals. He would get kicked out of group homes because of his violent temper, then he would be on the street, and the police would pick him up and take him to the mental hospital, and upon his release he would go to a new group home. The group home was supposed to make sure he took his medications, but when he got kicked out, his illness would again get out of control. The cycle of "group home—kicked out—arrested—committed to a mental facility—group home" became the norm.

The best thing that ever happened to John was that he was hospitalized at Central State in Petersburg, Virginia. There he was placed in a step-by-step program specifically for individuals with schizophrenia. That was the first and last time that anyone really focused on the illness and helped him to understand it. They educated him, and he really did well there. They taught him how to recognize the signs of when he was in trouble. When he came out of that program, he was assigned a caseworker, and he saw her on a regular basis.

Shortly after getting out of Central State, he moved into another group home, found a job, began taking night classes at a local junior college and was doing really well. He was working for a large church doing janitorial work. He loved that job. Then all of a sudden the group home said, "You are earning too much money. You have to quit your job."

We thought, "What are they doing here?" John was not even making minimum wage, it was something like thirty dollars a week. He loved the job; he was doing well at it. Why did they do that? It was a big turning point for him.

When he stopped working, he was lost. This was a very large group home. It had three floors and two people per room. The thing that was so hard was to see all those people just sitting around doing absolutely nothing. I know there are some who do not want to work, but there are a lot who could have benefited from work; it makes people feel good about themselves. The group home seemed more interested in continuing to receive government funding than in the welfare of our son.

When he was not in a group home, he was traveling all over the country bumming rides, getting day-labor jobs, panhandling to get money, and then traveling to the next town, where once again he would sleep in shelters and eat at soup kitchens. During this time he was really in an extreme state of schizophrenia. He would call us at all hours of the day and night from all over the country in a rage and claimed that variously the FBI or my employer or a close family friend was out to get him.

The last few months of his life are a total blank. In July 2002, just days before John's thirty-eighth birthday, four kids reportedly tried to rob him. John slapped his attacker with a newspaper and ran. The attacker shot him in the back; the bullet went through his heart. One of the kids was later arrested for a drive-by shooting, and the two remaining witnesses were threatened into changing their story. The police had to drop the case because of a lack of evidence. We believe it is all in God's hands, and we trust justice will one day be served.

The last several years of John's life were hell for him. He was always running, always afraid and so were we. We worried about him and where he was and our younger daughter was always fearful that he would show up and try to kill us. When he died, our first thought was that he was finally at peace. It probably seems cold, but I have to say that the shock and sadness of our son's death was accompanied by a sense of relief from the tension and fear that we all felt. He IS in a better place, and, frankly, so are we.

What is sad is that John was open to receiving help. After he was in Central State he did well for quite a while. For a while we thought we had finally found the answer. We did the best we could but we do believe the system failed our son. The group homes simply did not have enough qualified people to provide the level of care someone with severe mental illness needs. I think he would have benefited from a home that had a smaller, more intimate atmosphere where someone was truly working for his best interest and not just providing a roof over his head. Mental illness has seldom been handled well by society. I think that only a collective compassion guided by God's love can help—one soul at a time.

> *Mental illness has seldom been handled well by society. I think that only a collective compassion guided by God's love can help —one soul at a time.*

Dreams of William and John: Opportunities to work.

Dreams of Bob and Kathy: Quality mental-health care.

---

6 Dreams of Giving Back

Respect is sustained in the relationships in two related ways—by recognizing the gifts that guests bring to the relationship and by recognizing the neediness of the hosts . . . Hospitality is a two-way street.

—CHRISTINE POHL

Dorothy Day, the founder of the Catholic Worker Movement, writes, "The mystery of the poor is this: That they are Jesus, and what you do for them you do for Him."[1] She served hundreds of poor men and women in the slums of New York City, and through them she claimed to have encountered Christ. It seemed like such a bizarre suggestion. However, after my encounter in the Goochland Prison, I was beginning to understand something of the mystery of Christian hospitality and was curious to know more.

More than a year after my prison prayer asking God to bring me an "Abigail" on the outside, our church hosted CARITAS. CARITAS is the largest emergency-shelter program in Richmond, with a different local church hosting homeless individuals overnight for a week. I had signed up to serve one evening while the families were staying at my church, partly because I thought it would be good for my ten-year-old daughter to do this with me, and partly because I was still trying to understand the power of this practice called Christian hospitality. The weeks leading up to our church's hosting the homeless, I repeatedly encountered the same passage of Scripture—Matthew 25:40: "Truly I tell you, just as you did it to one of the least of these who are members of my family, you

1. Day, "The Mystery of the Poor."

did it to me" (NRSV). I heard it in the sermon the week before, it was the key verse in my daily-devotional book, and as I entered the church room that night, it was this verse that was painted over the doorframe. These signs made me think that in some way I would encounter Christ through this experience.

As the homeless families exited the bus that had brought them and entered the building, I began sizing them up, ranking them in order of potential Christ encounters. Those who smiled at me I moved high on the list, and those with a scowl went to the bottom of the list. The last woman to depart the bus was the only Caucasian woman in the shelter that night. Dreadlocks draped her head, but they were the strangest dreadlocks I have ever seen, with gum wrappers, pipe cleaners, pop tabs, and all sorts of colorful or shiny objects woven into them. She had a nose ring, tattoos on her hands, baggy pants, combat boots, and a big over-sized black T-shirt with a red anarchy sign and the words "Against All Authority" printed on it in a gothic font. Everything about this woman screamed, "Stay away!" And that is what I intended to do. I placed her at the bottom of my mental list—with a warning sign.

Later I found out that these women and their children had gotten up at 5:00 a.m. and traveled forty-five minutes by bus into the city, where they roamed the streets or sat in the basement of the church until 4:30 p.m., when they climbed back on the bus and were brought to my church. They were tired, and as I began making the rounds looking for my Christ encounter, trying to enter into conversation with them, I found that all they wanted was dinner and a bed. The night wore on, and I gave up trying to find Christ among the homeless. Apparently Dorothy Day had never met this particular group of homeless people!

Then the woman with the crazy hair did something quite unexpected. She invited all the children to come and make a "Thank-You Book" to give to the church. This woman, who had looked so scary to me earlier that evening was joined on the floor by six little artists who were drawing pictures of things they were thankful for. One drew a picture of pizza, another a pair of new tennis shoes, and another pictures of trees and a sun. Each had a story to tell, and the scary-looking lady listened attentively to each child. Have you ever noticed that little children are pretty good judges of character? As the children were finishing their artwork, the formerly scary lady's baby woke up. From the infant carrier, she lifted a tiny three-week-old baby girl. Looking at that sweet little face, I was shocked by the resemblance this child bore to my own daughter when she had been that age. I looked over at my ten-year-old daughter, who was giving horsey rides to some of the children, and longed for those early days.

I could stay away no longer. I had to see that baby. Plopping down on the floor next to the lady and her child, I said, "What a beautiful baby." She proceeded to share her story, starting with the words, "I am so thankful God locked me in jail so that now I can be the mother my daughter deserves." I had never heard anyone praise God for locking them in jail! This lady had my attention. She explained how she had gotten addicted to prescription drugs, which led to street drugs, which led to crime, which had landed my new friend, Stephanie, in jail. She had been released from prison just a few days before the baby was born, and with nowhere to go, she had found her way to the shelter. So here she sat thanking God for a cot to sleep on and for food and for a second chance. What I took for granted she saw as gifts directly from the hand of God to her. As she held that little baby, she said, "This time I am going to make it." I hardly knew her yet felt connected to her.

As I left the room a little voice inside my mind was asking, "What's going to happen to Stephanie and baby, Emma?"

I turned around and went back into the room and said, "I know this is kind of strange, but I really enjoyed visiting with you. Could I come visit you again?"

She said, "I do not have any friends or family here. I would really enjoy having someone to visit with."

I had gone that evening thinking I was the host and that Stephanie and her friends were our guests. However, Stephanie was the one who had extended Christian hospitality to me. She had given me the only thing she had to give: herself through her story. That is the mystery of Christian hospitality: it is always mutual. The guest becomes the host, and the host becomes the guest, and both are changed.

That is the mystery of Christian hospitality: it is always mutual. The guest becomes the host, and the host becomes the guest, and both are changed.

I visited Stephanie a few times in the day shelter, and then she got keys to her own apartment. I was as excited as she was. I was also afraid. The apartment was in the inner city; being from the suburbs, I knew little about the city except what I had seen on TV—and that was not comforting. It took me a week to find the courage to venture alone into the city to find her. I had my husband on the cell phone the entire time just in case there was foul play. He had tried to talk me out of it, but I was determined to find my new friend. Determined, but also terrified. When I finally reached her door, all my fear vanished when I heard her delighted yell: "Yay! You found me!" She threw the door open and gave me a warm embrace. No stranger, she was my sister.

Bubbling over with joy, Stephanie moved from room to room, showing me her apartment. "This is the dining room, this is the living room, this is the baby's room, and this is my room." We finished the tour of her tiny apartment, and I was speechless. I kept expecting to enter a room and find a bed or a couch or at least a chair, but instead every single room was bare. Her only possessions were a few articles of clothing. She had been in the apartment a week using her coat as a pillow while the baby slept in an infant carrier. I could not help myself and blurted, "Stephanie, where is all your stuff!"

She looked puzzled and said, "I don't need stuff, God got me this far, God will take care of the stuff."

Here I was, the seminary student, the minister in training, and all I could see was her lack. There she was, pointing to the only one who could truly meet her needs.

One thing I had learned from my study of Scripture was that God never works alone; God always works through people. To free the Israelites, God used Moses. To spread the Christian faith, God used the apostles. And to help rectify Stephanie's lack of material things, God would provide through someone else. No matter how much she prayed or believed, furniture would not fall from the sky. I stood there dumbfounded by the fact that in a city as wealthy as Richmond this mother and child had no bed on which to sleep, no dishes from which to eat, and no sofa on which to sit: and I knew somehow God was calling me to do something. I looked at her and said, "I do not know what I can do, but if I found some furniture for you and Emma, would that be O.K.?"

She smiled. "Wendy, that would be fine, but please do not worry about us."

But all the way home, I did worry about Stephanie and Emma. Worrying is something I am quite good at. Stephanie would have her hands full trying to teach me to live by as much faith as she had learned to live by. As soon as I got home, I composed an e-mail to my then forty Quest women who were members of my women's ministry. The e-mail said, "You are not going to believe this, but there is a woman sleeping on the floor and a baby sleeping in an infant carrier. I am going to leave my garage door open and in two days I am going to take to her whatever you donate." In two days we completely furnished Stephanie's apartment. I was overwhelmed by the generosity of my suburban neighbors, many of whom thanked me for finding a good home for their items. It is not that God has not provided for all God's children; it is simply that the stuff is a little misallocated. God had been storing Stephanie's blessings in the attics, in the garages, and under the beds of my suburban neighbors.

I am so thankful that my husband was able to meet Stephanie on the day we delivered the furniture to her. It prepared him for what was to come. She cried tears of joy the entire time and kept saying, "Why are you doing this? You do not even know me! If you knew me, you would not be doing this. I don't deserve this. I have never had things this nice before. Thank you."

The story could have ended there. Stephanie could have said, "Thank you, nice lady who gives away stuff. Now go away." But as God would have it, Stephanie's apartment was just down the road from my seminary, and she invited me to visit anytime. For the next several months, I regularly stopped by to see how she and Emma were doing. I watched her joy fade and her frustration grow into aggravation and depression. The change puzzled me.

Finally I said, "Stephanie, what's wrong? You are just not yourself."

She said, "Day after day I sit in this apartment with nothing to do. I can't afford childcare—and besides, no one will hire me with my record. I am scared. I am scared that if I do not do something, I am going to go crazy, or worse, I am going to go back to the streets."

I asked, "What is it you want to do with your life?"

She replied, "I just want to help people because so many people helped me." That is when it happened. Stephanie and I moved from mutual hospitality to shared mission.

I asked Stephanie to learn more about the needs of her neighbors. She found out that the little boy next door was seven and had never had a bicycle, so I sent out a request for a bike, and I got four bikes. I drove them to Stephanie, and she gave them away. Next, she learned that the lady upstairs needed a baby stroller. One e-mail yielded three strollers. Word got around my neighborhood that I knew people in need in the city, and people just started bringing things to my garage. I would load up the goodies, and Stephanie would find homes for them. I was Robin Hood, and she was Santa Claus, and we were having a great time blessing her neighborhood. Stephanie's smile returned, and she began to glow with a new hope as she found purpose and meaning by serving others.

Martha is a case manager for the shelter where I met Stephanie. Below, Martha shares some of the insights she has gleaned through her years working with families in poverty. Her experience echoes the findings of Ruby K. Payne, Philip E DeVol, and Terie Dreussi Smith, as shared in the book *Bridges Out of Poverty*: "Individuals leave poverty for one of four reasons: a goal or vision of something they want to be or have; a situation that is so painful that anything would be better; someone who "sponsors" them (an educator, mentor, or role model who shows them a different way or convinces them that they can live differently); or a specific talent or ability that provides an opportunity for them."[2]

Insights from Martha Patrick, a Shelter Case Manager

My mom was in social work, and my dad helped people get jobs, so helping others was always something I wanted to do. I have a degree in social work and started my career working with Child Protective Services, which was a trial-by-fire experience. I saw how some of the issues could have been prevented if I could have worked with the women earlier and helped them with relationship skills, counseling services, or mental-health services before they began neglecting their children, turning to drugs, or losing their children due to homeless-

2. Payne et al., *Bridges Out of Poverty*, 63.

ness. Back in 1986, when I first started in the field of social work, if you were a homeless parent, the authorities would take your children from you and put them in foster care. There were no family shelters back then. Today families are the fastest-growing segment of homeless people. Children are the fastest-growing demographic.[3]

I have encountered many people just like Stephanie during my time as a case manager. People are in a situation in which they have lost everything, and they are thankful to have anything. The longer I do this job; the more reasons I discover as to why people become homeless. There are certain things that are more devastating than others, such as drug use, which take much longer to recover from, and some people come back through the system time and time again until they finally get adequate treatment to break the cycle.

When they come into the shelter, families almost visibly sigh with relief. The burdens are lifted; they are not worrying about where they will sleep, what they will eat, whether Child Protective Services will take the children. All those worries are gone, and in the beginning they just sleep and sleep and sleep. When that primary need has been fulfilled, we then try to get them back to work. I always try to figure out what has led a person to this place of crisis, and try to get them to focus on those root issues.

While a lack of affordable housing options is the primary issue, the underlying issue is poor money management on the part of our clients. They got to this place because they did not pay their bills. While some of our clients were never taught how to take responsibility for their actions and did not have parents that modeled responsible living, for others there is a kind of rebelliousness that is hard to explain.

I see this particularly among the young women who already have a couple of children, who dropped out of school, who never got their GED, and who can barely hold down a job at a fast-food restaurant. They are angry. It never occurred to me that I would not go to college, but for these women no one is holding out the ideal for them that they can achieve more. No one said to these young ladies,

---

3. Coalition for the Homeless, "Who Is Homeless?"

"I can't wait to see you go to college." Among the poor there is such a focus on survival, on the day-to-day, from paycheck to paycheck. They can have dreams and goals, but often no one has talked to them about their potential.

As you can imagine, this cycle leads to depression, although some people who suffer from depression do not even know it; they just can't figure out why they can't get it together. For many the pain of depression and other mental health problems drive them to abuse substances or to seek out unhealthy relationships—which further fuel the cycle of poverty.

At any given time 70 to 80 percent of the clients in my caseload are suffering from depression or another form of mental illness to the point that it is impairing their ability to function. I strongly encourage all my clients to take advantage of counseling while they are in the shelter. We have figured out how best to access those systems, but if you do not know the process, it can be very hard. Even if they do have access, many will not use the services unless they have someone like me in their face, challenging them to get help. They do hate me sometimes, but they know I work for their own best interests.

Depression grows out of a sense of hopelessness. The most powerful thing we can give people is hope. Many of these women do not have dreams. A dream is a luxury our clients think they can't afford. However, with a dream comes hope, hope in a future that is better than today's reality. A dream is a powerful motivator.

However, with a dream comes hope, hope in a future that is better than today's reality. A dream is a powerful motivator.

If we can help our clients find their dream and set some realistic goals, something tangible to work for, we can help them break out of the cycle. They need someone who is going to help them find the path that leads to that dream, and someone who is going to cheer them along as they go, someone who will ensure they get the training and resources they need to succeed. Whether it is computer training, GED classes, help finding appropriate clothing for an interview, or being a listening ear when things are not going well, it is these simple things that keep them going. This kind of thing does not require social-work training; anyone can do it, and it is what is most needed. Our clients need confidence to get back out there and to keep on trying.

It is important in my occupation to maintain a professional distance. I can't get too attached to one particular client or family, because I know they will have to move on and therefore need the internal strength to manage without me. As for me, I will have to focus on the next client. Our clients need someone to walk alongside them, to be there for them as they make this transition, to be their encourager.

Stephanie's dream: To help others.

Martha's dream: To help women discover and live their dreams.

7 A Community Dreams

*Perhaps the greatest mistake commonly made by those who strive
to help the poor is the failure to see the assets and strengths that are
always present in people and their communities no matter how poor
they are.*

—RICHARD STEARNS

A few months into our Robin-Hood/Santa-Claus experiment, Stephanie
received a visit from her social worker, Robinette. When Robinette saw
all the stuff in Stephanie's apartment, she was alarmed. "Where did you
get all these things?" Stephanie said, "There is this nice lady and we are
giving it all away." Robinette was not satisfied; she wanted to meet me. It
did not take her long to figure out I was not a drug dealer or a thief, just a
little unorthodox. Stephanie and I shared our vision of helping people in
need, and she looked at me and said, "Wendy, Stephanie is not the only
formerly homeless person in Richmond sleeping on the floor. There are
dozens of individuals just like her. Could you and Stephanie help other
individuals who are exiting the shelters?" Stephanie and I looked at each
other uncertain what to say. We promised to pray about it.

I approached my Yada Yada group, the women in my Quest Women's
ministry, my pastor, my seminary professors, my fellow students, and
anyone else who would listen, and I asked them to pray. We knew we
could not store furniture in Stephanie's tiny apartment; we would need a
large space. One thing led to another, and we found ourselves at Highland
Park United Methodist Church (HPUMC).

Highland Park UMC began worshipping in the heart of the Highland Park community in 1892. In 1914, a Richmond newspaper called Highland Park "A progressive town with splendid schools, streets and fire fighting facilities. Civic pride is always at high tide. It's an ideal place to live."[1]

From its inception the church experienced steady growth until 1957. Several different building campaigns had resulted in three different buildings with more than twenty-five thousand square feet of space. In 1939 the church made history when Miss Lillian Russell, a member of Highland Park Church, became the first woman ever licensed to preach by the Virginia Conference. At its peak in 1957, Highland Park UMC was the fourth-largest church in the Virginia conference, with a membership of 2,200 people.

The church's history records the turning point:

> With the arrival of the 1960s, the all-white churches in Highland Park faced a new situation. The racial makeup of the community was rapidly changing, as white residents moved away and blacks moved in. The white congregations of four mainline Protestant denominations sold their buildings and moved elsewhere or merged with existing churches in other parts of the city. As white members of Highland Park Methodist moved away and the community underwent racial change, this church's membership began to decline in numbers. The question that had to be answered was whether the Methodist Church would follow the example of the other white congregations and leave Highland Park.
>
> The answer came in 1972 when 56% of the members responding to a questionnaire said they wanted the church to remain in the community. Of this 56%, 35% wanted the church to stay but to concentrate on serving its own members. In any event, a majority favored remaining in Highland Park, and that course was followed.[2]

By the time I discovered HPUMC in the summer of 2004, the congregation had dwindled to about twenty active parishioners. The existing congregation had closed off entire floors and was using only a small portion of the available space. The boiler had gone out and the air conditioning units did not work, but if we wanted it, the congregation

1. Jones and Nottingham, *Highland Park United Methodist Church.*
2. Ibid

said we could use the old Sunday-school wing to house furniture free of charge. Walking those halls was like walking in a ghost town. The inside of that church reflected much of what one found in the community. Abandoned buildings. Boarded-up homes. A sense of loss permeated the air. Both the church and the community were a far cry from their original splendor.

Despite its shortcomings, I loved that old building. While others saw only the peeling paint and the broken windows, I saw the potential this enormous space held. We began doing biweekly distributions. We collected all the furniture we could over two weeks then put it on the church lawn and gave it to those in need. There was no real process. However, we did require that everyone hear the story. I told them how this started because a homeless woman wanted to give back. We urged everyone to "take what you need, but then please come back and help us."

The number of individuals who came back to help amazed me. People would arrive at 9:00 a.m. and often stay until 4:00 p.m.: partially because of the growing numbers of people requesting assistance, and partially because we all enjoyed each other's company. We began providing lunch, and our numbers grew higher. Out of curiosity, individuals from the surrounding neighborhood ventured onto church property. They asked, "Is this some kind of yard sale?" "No," I would say. "We are giving everything away to homeless families. Would you like to help?" Some immediately turned and left, but on occasion some said, "Sure. What do you need?" We formed an interesting crew: me, the minister in training, a bunch of formerly homeless individuals, some of my Quest women from the suburbs, and a few random neighbors who joined in to support the cause.

It was during our time in Highland Park that God blessed us with two grandparents. Mrs. Georgiana came with her daughter, who was in need of furniture. The prospect of having someplace to go and some-

> *I told them how this started because a homeless woman wanted to give back. We urged everyone to "take what you need, but then please come back and help us." The number of individuals who came back to help amazed me.*

thing to do with her time thrilled Georgiana. At seventy, she is the feisty mother of twelve and grandmother of thirty-five. She reminded me of my friend Opal from the adult home: a sharp mind and a lot of life left in her. She lives in public housing and watches as her neighbors rob and even kill one another for drugs and personal gain, but every week she pushes her walker up the hill so that she can spend hours organizing donations and helping those in need in our community. Embrace Richmond, the organization we founded to help people in need is a safe haven for her, a place where the common good is the goal. Her grandchildren and my children spend summers together, and all have learned how much alike they are despite their different skin color and economic means.

Our second grandparent was Mr. Tony Brickhouse, whom we all just call Brickhouse. Brickhouse came to Embrace with his granddaughter, who had just exited the shelter. He stood watching while a bunch of middle-aged women wrestled furniture into any vehicle available. We were strapping mattresses to tops of small cars and smashing couches into minivans. Our greatest challenge was transporting all the furniture that was pouring into the ministry. Each week, Aileen and I drove our husbands' trucks from the suburbs, loaded two and three layers high, and delivered as much furniture as we could at the end of the day. However, families without transportation waited for hours while we distributed furniture at the church to those who had their own vehicles.

As we loaded Brickhouse's granddaughter's things into his 1974 Ford pickup truck, I commented, "I wish everyone had a grandfather as kind as you!"

Brickhouse smiled and said, "Call me anytime." I never forget an offer for help. He has been delivering furniture for me ever since. Like my old friend Mr. Peterson, the taxicab driver, Brickhouse knows the streets of Richmond; and like Georgiana, he wanted to encourage this countercultural experiment in hospitality.

During our time at HPUMC we started to work closely with the battered-women's shelter. Two very special women joined our growing team during this time: Katy and Rosalind. Both were victims of domestic violence. Rosalind was the mother of four children; she had fled New York City with absolutely nothing. Rosalind remembers her decision to come to Richmond:

I was going from one shelter to another in New York City after fleeing from the abuse inflicted upon me by the father of my children. The last shelter I was in was in the city, and their father found me because I used my EPT card at the supermarket. I didn't want to risk the lives of the other families at the shelter, so I went back to him. After I had endured much abuse, we got into another huge fight, and I called the police again. One of the officers was very rude and simply said, "We cannot find him, and if you call us again we are going to take your children away from you." I didn't know what to do. I endured two more years of abuse. I felt I had no voice, which made me weak in spirit, mind, and body in addition to the physical wounds. There seemed to be no way out. That's when I started to use drugs heavily without my family knowing. I prayed to God, I assumed for the last time, as I contemplated suicide. In that hour, I believe he heard me and gave me endurance, saying, "My weeping child, endure for one night but joy cometh in the morning." I felt God directing me to call the hotline and trust Him that whatever they had available was for me, no matter where it was. I did just that. I was told there were two beds at the YWCA in Richmond. I called my uncle, and he paid the tickets. I got on the bus with four diapers, two biscuits, six pieces of chicken, four children, and a broken heart, and God has carried us all this way.

Rosalind knew no one in Richmond and had no idea how she and her children were going to survive. She immediately went to the shelter expecting to be in her own home within a few weeks. Eight months later, Rosalind got her keys. She moved into a home in Highland Park and volunteered every week. Rosalind transformed before our eyes. She came to the ministry beaten down and uncertain of what the future held for her and her children. Over the next few months, she gained confidence and started encouraging other volunteers from the shelters saying, "Hang in there. It will all work out."

Rosalind encouraged Katy to join us. We nicknamed Katy "bulldog" because she was the toughest woman I had ever met. Managing furniture distribution, I tend to be a bit of a pushover. Katy, on the other hand, does not let anyone leave the building with more than they need. One day, two large men tried to take some beds from our courtyard. Katy looked at me and said, "Let me handle this." She ran down the stairs and stopped the men as they loaded our mattresses into their truck. I do not know what she said, but when she pointed at the mattresses and then to the sidewalk, these would-be thieves obeyed and returned their stolen booty. Katy also moved into a home in Highland Park just a few streets from the church. She worked nights and helped us during the day.

I guess that first year in HPUMC was the "honeymoon" phase of our ministry. While things were sometimes tough, it did not seem to matter. We were doing something new and exciting, and everyone on the team seemed to enjoy one another. Aileen, Stephanie, Georgiana, Rosalind, Brickhouse, Katy, and I would never have met one another in the normal course of life, but through this little experiment that we had named Embrace Richmond in honor of Frances of Goochland Correctional Facility, God brought us all together. For a season, that was enough.

> *From the ruins of racially fueled devastation, which had brought this community to the edge of utter destruction, something new was bubbling to the surface. God was honoring the prayers of our ancestors.*

From the ruins of racially fueled devastation, which had brought this community to the edge of utter destruction, something new was bubbling to the surface. God was honoring the prayers of our ancestors. During our time at HPUMC, I was given the church's history to read and was particularly moved by its description of a former pastor, the Reverend Edgar J. Nottingham III.

Reverend Edgar J. Nottingham III served as pastor of Highland Park UMC from 1974 to 1980—during some of the most challenging years in the church's 115-year existence, as Nottingham describes here:

> During the past two decades Highland Park Church, has been tempted to fall into the error of setting up a false dilemma: On the one hand to focus exclusively on nurturing and enhancing the lives of persons within the membership; or, on the other hand, to see herself primarily as a social agency called to serve the physical needs of the financially deprived in the community by feeding the hungry, clothing the naked and releasing the captives.

It has long seemed significant to the writer of this sketch that when the congregation planned the sanctuary, words from the Prophet Isaiah were carved over the entrance: "MINE HOUSE SHALL BE A HOUSE OF PRAYER FOR ALL PEOPLE." The experience of all branches of the Church Universal demonstrates there seems to be a built-in resistance to achieving this goal.[3]

In a letter to the editor of *Richmond Magazine* in 1976, Rev. Nottingham wrote: "My concern is that I share the conviction that the philosophy guiding the future development of the Capital City cannot and should not be that of the nineteenth century: 'White is white and black is black and never the two shall meet.'"[4]

Nottingham was fighting a losing battle. He stood up for what was right in a cultural tide that swept away almost his entire congregation. He was not alone. In 1976, Highland Park UMC was one of 116 churches in the Virginia Conference recognized as being in communities undergoing significant racial and/or economic change.

Nottingham retired after six years at Highland Park UMC and forty-two years as a Methodist minister. He leaves us with these words: "During these years of transition there have been two beacon lights to guide the congregation when many have seen danger and threatening darkness. First, the words of Isaiah, the Prophet of the Exile: 'MINE HOUSE SHALL BE A HOUSE OF PRAYER FOR ALL PEOPLE.' Second, the faith and commitment to Christian ministry expressed in the experience of Paul the Apostle to the Gentiles: 'A wide door for effective work has opened to me, and there are many adversaries.' (I Corinthians 16:9)."[5]

While I never had the privilege of meeting Reverend Nottingham, I feel a kinship with him. I think his spirit continued to live on in that church in Highland Park. I think he would have been proud to see our early Embrace crew, black and white, rich and poor, urban and suburban, all working together to be a blessing to others. Thank you, Rev. Nottingham for fighting the good fight; for standing up for what is right.

3. Ibid
4. Ibid
5. Ibid

Reflections from Tony Brickhouse

I am sixty-four years old, and I have seen a lot of changes in my life. Back in the '60s, '70s, and even '80s, white people and black people were kept far apart in this city. Wendy and I never would have met back in those days. She never would have come into my neighborhood, and I knew better than to go into hers. If a white woman had come in my neighborhood back in that day, I would have stayed far from her. All she would have had to do is yell, "Rape!" and everyone in the vicinity would have been hauled off to jail.

People don't believe it today, but back in the '70s black men did not walk down the main streets of the city. We knew how far we could go. We knew not to go into Oregon Hill; that was where the rednecks lived—the ones flying the confederate flags. That was a dangerous place for us to go. We just stayed far away from there. Even today you have some of that ingrained racism in parts of this city. Everyone was fighting everyone back then, and I could tell what color you were simply by what neighborhood you came from.

Fear swept through this city, driven by propaganda that made every white woman fear the black man. That was the norm. There is still is so much fear of the other.

I am telling you the truth. Thirty or forty years ago, Wendy would not have wanted to be in the same room with me. I was one mean dude. I scare myself just thinking about how mean I was. You did not have to do anything. If you just looked at me wrong or bumped me, I would go on the attack. I was an angry and frustrated young man.

Then I got into some trouble and had to go see this white lady who was with the American Civil Liberties Union. Back then, the ACLU helped people who could not afford attorneys. At the time the black/white thing was really crazy.

This lady looked at me and said, "You are anti-white, anti-Christ, anti-Brickhouse, anti-everything."

I looked at her and I said "So what!" and she looked at me and said, "I have not done anything to you, why are you so angry with me?"

Right then something clicked in my head. She said, "I am here to help you." I realized that that lady was a nice lady. I realized I actually liked her. That encounter did something to me, and I started to see people, especially white people, differently.

Back in 2005, the day my granddaughter called me to help her move out of the shelter, I was shocked that she had not told me she was homeless. I had no idea that she and her children were in the shelter. She felt like I would have gotten upset with her, so she kept it from me.

When I first pulled up at Highland Park UMC that day, it just looked like mass confusion. All the ladies with all these little kids were all running around grabbing furniture, pushing it into cars, no men anywhere. And I thought, "What have I gotten myself into?" And all these young ladies saw me with a truck and they kept coming up to me and saying, "Can you help me move my stuff?"

And I said, "I just came to help my granddaughter." I honestly did not know what was going on. I just stood back and watched, and I realized these ladies needed help real bad.

When Wendy asked if I would help the ladies, I said, "As long as they pay for the gas, I will help. Just give me a call." That is how I got connected with Embrace. I bet I have delivered over two hundred households worth of furniture since that day. Over the years I met some lovely people and some not-so-lovely people. I met some that appreciated the help, and others that were not so appreciative. But what is amazing is that none of them ever forget me. No matter where I go in the city now, I will hear, "Hi, Mr. Brickhouse!" and I wonder, who is that? Then I realize it is one of the families I helped through Embrace. I don't think they really recognize me: I think they remember my old, ugly 1974 pickup truck.

For most of my life, I had been down the road of take, take, take, take, take, take, take. That had been my life. I had never matured beyond that. All I cared about was what I was going to get out of the deal. And I never advanced. I never got anywhere, and I always wondered why.

Then when I got the food truck and started selling food in the housing projects, there were always one or two kids who did not have any money. So, one time I gave two of them some food and made them promise they would not tell the others. Then later of course more and more of them came, but more of them had money, and it seemed the more I gave, the more I got.

So when Wendy asked me to come back and give, I thought, well let me give this a try. And I found out that the more I gave, the more I got. Then when I ran into people who needed help, Wendy gave me things that I could give to others in need. Just like last week with the young student that asked me for a computer monitor. She asked me, I asked Wendy, and Wendy helped me out so that I could help the young girl. That is why I keep coming back, because it works when we all give just a little. It's like a cycle, and everyone gets what they need when everyone plays their part.

For three years since I started helping Embrace, God has really been looking out for me and that old truck. That truck should have long ago fallen apart. It is a 1974 Ford Ranger pickup truck. It is the Ranger back when the Ranger was a full-size truck. That truck is thirty-four years old! All I do is put in gas and oil and change the tires, and it is still running and still delivering furniture. I wonder now why it took me so long to learn to give. There really is something to that. Whether people believe or not, it is true that if you give, you do get more back.

Something else that happened to me was that I stopped wanting for things. No one believes me when I tell them that. They say "How can you stop wanting for things?" And I say, "I just do not want any more. Everything that I have asked for, I have received." Now I just sit back and think, "How can I help others?" It is strange. I do not want for anything, but when I need something, there it is right in front of me. It is so freeing to be free of want. That is the gift of giving; it breaks the cycle of always wanting more. I wish young people today would learn that lesson earlier in their lives than I did.

> *It is so freeing to be free of want. That is the gift of giving; it breaks the cycle of always wanting more.*

Tony Brickhouse's dream: That more people
would embrace the gift of giving.

8 I Have a Dream of Reconciliation

People are poor not just because of their sins;
they are poor because of our sins.

—SHANE CLAIBORNE

As Embrace Richmond's ministry took root in Highland Park, the reality of the separation between wealthy and poor, and black and white, struck me as dramatic. The city's history of racial segregation was still fueling much of the current separation. On August 28, 1963, Dr. Martin Luther King stood in front of the Lincoln Memorial and delivered his "I have a Dream" address, saying:

> Five score years ago, a great American, in whose symbolic shadow we stand today, signed the Emancipation Proclamation. This momentous decree came as a great beacon of hope to millions of Negro slaves who had been scared in the flames of withering injustice. It came as a joyous daybreak to end the long night of their captivity. But one hundred years later, the Negro still is not free; one hundred years later, the life of the Negro is still sadly crippled by the manacles of segregation and the chains of discrimination; one hundred years later the Negro lives on a lonely island of poverty in the midst of a vast ocean of material prosperity: one hundred years later the Negro is still languishing in the corners of American society and finds himself in exile in his own land.[1]

As I read Dr. King's words, the phrase "the Negro lives on a lonely island of poverty in the midst of a vast ocean of material prosperity" de-

1. King, "I have a dream."

scribed perfectly the Highland Park community. I realized that in some ways, the Civil War still raged in the capital of the Confederacy.

As my family and I pursued our move from Houston to Richmond, realtors warned my husband and me to steer clear of the city. They told us crime was terrible, and the schools were unacceptable. So we settled in a mostly white community called Woodlake. Highland Park, by contrast, was predominantly African American. Were these stark divisions new to me, or had I just begun to notice them? Perhaps moving to a new culture awakened me to the segregation, poverty, and violence that I had ignored in Houston.

Just months after we moved to Richmond, one particular incident opened my eyes to the undercurrent of racial injustice in my new home. One miserably hot day in August I was helping a church with face painting for the kids at the county fair. I looked up from finishing a child's face to find a sweaty, balding, bare-chested, drunken man standing in my line. His breath reeked of alcohol, and he said, "I want a confederate flag painted on my face so them n–––– will know not to mess with me."

I stared at him, thinking he was joking and trying to get a rise out of me. He was not. I informed him that I did not know how to paint a Confederate flag, which was true—but only part of the reason I refused to honor his request. He became belligerent. As his sweaty face turned red in anger, he stepped toward me. I looked around for someone to come to my defense. However, my fellow face-painting volunteers seemed unaffected by his request, and then a woman stepped forward and agreed to give him what he wanted. Satisfied, he left our ministry outpost with the confederate flag running down his face as the sweat washed parts of it onto his chest.

I was disgusted by the whole encounter, but the rest of this native Richmond team didn't seem to notice the sick statement that this man had made. I wanted the team to stop and pray for this disgusting bigot, but the others had become used to this sort of thing.

I had grown up in the South and had heard the *n* word used in vile ways before, but the context of this encounter profoundly affected me. I was there as a minister, and the front of our booth displayed the name of the church. For me, that made this space sacred, and the man's racial insult an affront to God. This encounter was the first sign that something was different about my new home.

I will never forget taking my daughters into the city after I began working in Highland Park. The number of abandoned buildings and people hanging out on street corners, and the graffiti and trash that littered the streets alarmed my then-six-, -eight-, and -ten-year-old daughters. My middle daughter asked, "Why do all the black people live here?" How do you explain generational poverty to an eight-year-old?

I asked her, "How would they leave?"

She said, "In their car." She was shocked when I informed her that most do not have cars. A city bus sped past, and she pointed and proudly announced, "They could ride the bus!" When I informed her that the bus does not go out into the county, with even more concern she asked, "Why not?"

All I could say was, "I wish I knew."

My eight-year-old easily identified just one of the systems creating a barrier in our city: transportation. Add poor schools and lack of employment to the equation, and it becomes obvious that the advice of my middle-class father to "pull yourself up by your bootstraps" was not enough for many to break the cycle of poverty.

My daughter also recognized that this entire community was black. Race is like a giant elephant sitting in the corner of the room when a discussion of poverty in Richmond arises. A newspaper reporter who wanted to do a series of stories on homelessness in Richmond interviewed me and asked me to provide him with names of homeless individuals that he could interview, and asked that the list contain a good deal of diversity in terms of age, race, marital status, and gender. I listed all the participants in our program whose stories would shed light on the challenges facing the homeless population and was proud of myself for coming up with a list that included every possible segment of homelessness (domestic violence, substance abuse, mental illness, and formerly incarcerated individuals). I also provided him with a diversity of ages and gender and marital status. But my list was lacking in one area: racial diversity. From the hundreds of households we had served, I could only name a handful of participants who were not African American. At that moment I realized that if I wanted to understand the true challenges in our city, I had to understand race and racism and how they contribute to poverty.

John Perkins, in his book *Beyond Charity*, writes, "Because race has been such a major player in our history, any attempts to solve the problems of our cities will mean, first, acknowledging the race problem instead of denying that it is a factor and, second, planning our strategies to anticipate the wild card of race. Otherwise race will continue to be an obstacle with enough emotional power to divide and conquer."[2]

My daughter assumed that black people choose to live in the inner city, but they often have no choices. Today race is not the question it was in 1963; the issue is economics. At what point are we going to own the fact that we (those with the power to create systems) have perpetuated systems initially designed to build a barrier of separation between us and them? From laws designed to prevent desegregation of schools to the development of public-housing projects, an honest reading of our history clearly demonstrates the level of racial tension in the region and the lengths to which those in power went to ensure that "white is white, and black is black, and never the two shall meet." We cannot say, that's in the past, and pretend unjust laws do not have an impact still felt today. These systems caused tremendous damage to the generations while they were in place. Tony Campolo, in *Revolution and Renewal*, puts it this way: "We are dealing with what sociologists have labeled 'systemic evil'—social, economic, and political structures and policies that, once created seem to have a life of their own."[3]

Many of Richmond's poorer African American residents have been raised in what I have heard referred to as "economic concentration camps." Generations of racial prejudice and injustice have bred a level of hopelessness that has replaced the white man as the chief oppressor.

> *Generations of racial prejudice and injustice have bred a level of hopelessness that has replaced the white man as the chief oppressor.*

While some whites still hold deep-seated racial views like those of the drunken Confederate-flag worshiper, I believe most residents of our city want to see racial diversity across the entire city. However, many are unwilling to admit that the ill effects of racially motivated

2. Perkins, *Beyond Charity*, 5.
3. Campolo, *Revolution and Renewal*, 45.

decisions made long ago are still felt by those caught in the trap of generational poverty.

Richmond has a significant number of public housing complexes. A majority of families in public-housing communities live below the poverty line. At the same time, Richmond is home to some of the nation's wealthiest communities. More than forty years after Dr. King's address, "the Negro *still* lives on a lonely island of poverty in the midst of a vast ocean of material prosperity."[4]

A year prior to moving into Highland Park, I met Martha Rollins. She is hard to miss: she is a sixty-six-year-old Caucasian woman with beautiful, long white hair, who set out to bring diversity back into the Highland Park community by creating economic opportunities and racial reconciliation. She is the founder and executive director of Boaz & Ruth (www.boazandruth.com).

Reflections from Martha Rollins

I was born in the small town of Martinsville, Virginia. It was Patrick Henry's homeplace—a place with his fierce spirit of independence, a place that was still fighting the Civil War. My class of 1961 yearbook theme was "The Old South," and it spoke of happy, lazy days on the plantation, being served mint juleps by "attentive Negro servants." I saw racial inequities—black waiting rooms, segregated lunch counters, and blacks restricted to seats at the back of the bus. My father was a successful businessman and mine was a third-generation textile family. Being Presbyterian, I learned faith as a call: "I will bless you so that you will be a blessing" (Genesis 12:2).

From 1961 to 1968, I attended Duke University, graduating with a Bachelor in Arts with distinction in religion, and a Master of Arts in teaching. During my first three years, Duke was all white except for the maids and janitors, who silently worked while we were in class. Until my senior year in college, none of the schools I attended were integrated.

During the summer of 1963, I did an internship at the Henry Street Settlement House in New York City. Those who worked there

4. King, "I have a dream," emphasis added.

provided basic social services and helped refugees get settled into the community—initially European and Jewish immigrants and then blacks who sought refuge in the north. There I worked for my first black boss and had a black roommate. For the first time, inequality had a face, a name, and a story.

During my time in New York, I heard Malcolm X speak at Abyssinian Baptist Church in Harlem. There were five of us that day, and we were the only white people in the church. Malcolm X took the stage, his words echoing through the sanctuary with such anger as he condemned the "White Wolf" and called his audience to resist efforts aimed at racial reconciliation. Sitting there surrounded by such a spirit of anger, I felt a heightened need to fight for peace and reconciliation. While this experience shaped me, it was not a sudden transformation. It is kind of like Moses. Moses did not all of the sudden decide to free the people. He saw the injustice, reacted, retreated, and then argued with God about his role in freeing the people. I continued to see racial and economic injustice but began asking the questions, "Why? And how do I fit into the solution?"

During my time at Duke I was also privileged to hear Dr. Martin Luther King Jr. speak on two separate occasions, and the experiences strengthened my own desire for equality and unity while still honoring our diversity.

In 1970, my husband and I moved to Richmond, Virginia—the capital of the Confederacy. Along Monument Avenue, statues of Confederate generals stand proudly facing the north, symbolically protecting their way of life. When I inquired about a house I had seen in the Carillon area, the realtor told me "You don't want to live there. It's a changing neighborhood." I am thankful I ignored that realtor's advice; it was that neighborhood that changed me and allowed me to finally discover how I could be part of the solution.

We were the first white family to purchase a house since the Carillon area had been "broken" (I would now call it "fixed.") a year earlier when the first black family had moved in. The day we moved into the house, the realtor said, "When the neighborhood 'goes' in five years, you ought to be able to get your money out." By "goes," he meant, "turns into an all-black neighborhood." He envisioned crime, abandoned buildings, and a dramatic drop in our property values. He was forecasting for my beautiful neighborhood what had happened all across the city.

I lay awake the first night imagining our house turned into low-income flats. The next morning I thought, "I am not going to let that happen." I realized that the realtor's forecast would likely happen unless something changed. However, I shared Dr. King's dream of living in harmony with my black neighbors, and I desperately wanted to live that vision. I knew that the key was to change the way people (in this case my neighbors) thought about one another. So I went out and started meeting my neighbors.

When Imogene Draper, a black neighbor my age, said, "I am from a little town you probably never heard of—Martinsville," I comprehended at a deeper level the unspoken reality and consequence of centuries of enforced racial separation and inequality. Racial separation would have kept me and Imogene separated forever had I allowed fear to keep me out of the Carillon area. As neighbors banding together, we formed the Carillon Civic Association and discovered "the power of we" and set out to bring social change.

During this time, my neighbors and I worked on an entrepreneurial venture to connect people across cultural lines. Arts in the Park made the entire city aware of our neighborhood as we fought against under-the-table racial real-estate steering. Arts in the Park is a now a thriving event drawing thousands of people from across the East Coast. In the 1970s the Carillon area was selected by the Ford Foundation as one of three successfully integrated neighborhoods in the country—and the only one in the South. All my black neighbors took on the role of "cross-cultural mentors," willingly sharing their knowledge and friendship with me and my husband, Randy.

In 1972 I borrowed money, rented a building for eighty-five dollars a month, purchased antiques, and told my husband at dinner that night that I was opening an antique shop. I had a vision for furniture restoration: I saw people restoring furniture in the natural, as they themselves were being restored in the spiritual. I observed the economic inequity, as very wealthy whites came in the front door to shop, and very poor blacks came in the back door, trying to make a meager living. During those years, I knew that I wanted to make a difference by using this experience to work for social change.

Finally in 2002, at the age of fifty-nine, it all began. A founding board of six women helped launch Boaz & Ruth training store in Highland Park. In the beginning it was Lloyd Price, myself, and five trainees operating the program and running the store.

We did not choose Highland Park; it chose us. Councilwoman Ellen Robertson offered me the use of an abandoned fire station in Highland Park to launch the program. I told Ellen, "We don't want to be in Highland Park; it's too dangerous." I remember hearing in my spirit as I said, No, I won't go there, echoes of Jonah's saying no to God, and I had a vision of a big fish swimming toward me. I knew right away that I had spoken the wrong words. The next week, God provided a large donation of designer furniture: our first donation. I had nowhere to put the donations, so I called Ellen back and accepted her offer.

I started attending a women's prayer group in the community. Within a few months of praying with these women, I knew God was showing me that we could impact not only the lives of those who would come to the training program but the entire neighborhood if we strategically placed our resources here where they were so desperately needed. So God took the vision of starting a job-training program for people who needed a second chance, and added to the vision a commitment to community transformation in Highland Park.

My first idea was to call the store Gleanings. However, as I was rereading the story in the book of Ruth, I realized that the theme in the book of Ruth was not "leftovers" but the power of relationships. In the biblical story we encounter Boaz, who on the surface had more than he needed, and Ruth, who on the surface had less than she needed. As they came together across racial, economic, and geographic lines, the world was changed. Through their union, Christ would eventually enter the world. Part of the vision behind B&R—Boaz & Ruth—is that if we come together across racial, economic, and geographic divisions, the same power that birthed Jesus is available to us. Everyone is a Boaz—with gifts, and everyone is Ruth—with needs.

The most important word in our name is the word *and*; it's all about connecting.

By 2005, we had added a second store, a café, catering, repair and restoration, home repair, furniture moving, and eBay sales. In December 2007, Firehouse 15—Shops and Restaurant—opened, as well as a used clothing store: all in the heart of Highland Park. The staff had increased to fourteen; trainees and graduates working at B&R numbered forty.

More than being about providing services, I think our presence has brought hope, peace, and hospitality. It is about welcoming God's presence into our outpost. Our one desire is to be what God called us to be, and to do so with great courage. We know that "perfect love casts out fear," so we continually have to choose love, not fear. The people who have come to support us have had to choose love, not fear. There have been a number of murders in the community, one of which happened on our front doorstep on September the 11th of 2004, and five more in the intersection across from Boaz & Ruth. It continues to be hard, but we continue to choose love, not fear. Our courage has helped our neighbors break out of their prisons of fear. One of our neighbors shared recently that she has been in the neighborhood eleven years, and that this past summer was the first time she had ever felt safe enough to sit on her front porch. Her feeling of safety came from the men from B&R, who live next door. Fear, mistrust, and greed are the things that keep us from achieving reconciliation, and prevent us from practicing Christian hospitality.

> *We know that "perfect love casts out fear," so we continually have to choose love, not fear.*

Martha's dream: To see God finish the dream that has grown out of Boaz & Ruth—making Highland Park a healthy village where there is safe, affordable housing and job opportunities in the community. I also hope my successor will help to take the Boaz & Ruth model into other cities.

---

9 Dreams Lost

After decades of entrenched material poverty, many communities suffer from a poverty of spirit as well.
—RICHARD STEARNS

Highland Park's violent reputation was well earned. Embrace Richmond's honeymoon there ended one sunny August day in 2005 when gunfire erupted. I had started Shine, a ministry for preteen girls from my neighborhood in the suburbs. That day we had about twenty young girls helping distribute furniture. The shooter was standing directly across the street and was firing the gun toward the front of the church where one of my clients was attempting to load her vehicle.

The shooter lowered the gun and ran into the house directly across from the church. Apparently, our client's son had gotten into a fistfight with another boy from the neighborhood, and a friend had gone into the house to get a gun to intimidate our clients who were not from the community. True: the shots were fired over the young man's head, but none of this made me feel any safer.

I had never heard gunfire or seen anyone wielding a gun in broad daylight. That bullet was intended to intimidate one young African American boy from the wrong side of town, but it blasted a hole through my ministry. The bridge of trust that I had been building for over a year suddenly collapsed.

This was the first really difficult challenge to our ministry. Should we stay in Highland Park, or should we leave? We realized that the gap separating the roughest inner-city community from one of the wealthiest suburban neighborhoods was just too large a gap for us to bridge without a safe place to meet in the middle. Those gunshots also began to awaken me to how difficult this bridge-building task would prove to be.

During this same time, another bridge was beginning to crumble. Stephanie and I had built a friendship and had been serving together on a regular basis for almost a year. Baby Emma was now walking and would run through the halls of Highland Park UMC, her laughter a regular reminder of why we did what we did. Then Stephanie's husband returned home from jail, and overnight everything changed. She had been so hopeful before Joe got home. He would make her life complete. But after Joe came home, Stephanie began to fade from the Embrace community, coming more sporadically and making excuses for why she could not attend: "Emma is sick, I am sick, Joe is sick."

It was Emma's first birthday, and we had a celebration planned. This time her excuse was "Joe needs me." What did that mean? He was a grown man. Their relationship was baffling to me. I later saw it for what it was: intense codependency. However, at the time, I just thought it was immaturity and hoped she would outgrow it.

Unfortunately on Emma's birthday, I realized just how far Stephanie had slipped from us. I called and offered to bring her the leftover cake. She began to cry and said, "Please, would you mind?" When I arrived, I was shocked by her appearance. Her eyes were lifeless, her body frail, and her face was covered with pink blotches. As she took hold of the birthday cake; tears began to stream down her face. The half-eaten cake had fallen off the seat of the car. Mangled and broken, it somehow represented the hope Stephanie had lost. She said, "Thank you for the cake. It is all we have to celebrate Emma's birthday." The life she had dreamt of had vanished, and she was once again caught in the trap of addiction that would lead to pain and destruction.

As I drove off, she stood in that parking lot holding that pathetic cake. That image in my rearview mirror would haunt me for years to come. Shortly thereafter, Stephanie vanished from my life: so much potential, so much intelligence, so many opportunities—all thrown away.

Two days before Christmas Stephanie was arrested for shoplifting. The jail waiting room was packed on Christmas Eve as I waited for more than two hours to see her. She tried to be pleasant, but her body was being racked with withdrawal pains from heroin. My ten-minute visit seemed more than Stephanie could bear. She asked the guard to take her back to her cell. Over the next several days, I received calls from both Stephanie and Joe begging me to bail her out. It was so hard to tell them no.

Watching Aileen walk beside Via in her recovery, I naively thought that if I just loved, accept-

> *I naively thought that if I just loved, accepted, supported, and prayed for Stephanie, she would make it. I had no idea how much power addiction had over her.*

ed, supported, and prayed for Stephanie, she would make it. I had no idea how much power addiction had over her. But most of all I underestimated the addiction she had to her husband. She told me that she would rather have nothing and live under a bridge than to live without Joe. I had thought that in a few months we would be able to reverse the ill effects of Stephanie's twelve-year addiction.

Likewise I naively thought that in a short period of time we could reverse the years of decay at Highland Park UMC. Shortly after the shooting, the congregation voted to close its doors and sell the building. The honeymoon was over, and the future of Embrace Richmond, like that of the homeless families we served, was uncertain.

My friend Sharon is no stranger to addiction and the interrelationship between addiction and codependency. Through her own painful journey, Sharon learned that no amount of human effort can save another person. I wish Sharon had been around to help Stephanie break free from codependency.

Insights from Sharon

I was the second child out of four in a strict Irish Catholic family. My older sister, whom I was very close to, became pregnant when she was sixteen, and I immediately went into caregiver mode trying to help my family cope. My father was so angry at her that he initially threw her out of the house. My mother was distraught over the loss of her daughter and insisted that my sister and the baby be allowed to live in the house. Eventually, my family adjusted, but I think somehow that experience catapulted me into this need to "get it right."

My parents would say to me, "You are not going to do this to us are you? You have to be the 'good' one." When I was a teen, that became my job: to be the "good girl" and do what is "right." I have lived that way most of my life. I had to be the best mom, the best wife, the best employee, the best Catholic; always seeking to please others.

When I got out of high school, I went to work for a corporation in Manhattan as a mail clerk and worked my way up over the next fifteen years into a management position. I married a good Irish Catholic boy, moved to Richmond, and had two children. After my children were born, I began to ask myself "Who is this man I am married to?" I had never really gotten to know him, and I realized that we really did not like one another. I had been so consumed by my career and climbing the corporate ladder, that the marriage was just one more thing on my to-do list. The marriage ended, and I found myself a single mother in a new city—all alone. My divorce was particularly hard on my father. I had failed him.

Shortly after my divorce, I met the man of my dreams. He was an attractive, educated, professional who swept me off my feet. We had so much in common, and he adored my children. He was the sweetest, kindest gentleman I had ever met. I could not believe how fortunate I was to find such an amazing man.

I will never forget our wedding night. My husband got really drunk, and when something went wrong with our hotel room, he got so angry with the hotel clerk that they called the police! So here I was on my wedding night, watching the cops interrogate Mr. Wonderful. This was the first of many incidents of this nature. To the outside world, everything was wonderful, and everyone thought I was so lucky to have such a great guy, but behind closed doors, our marriage was falling apart. It did not take me long to realize that he was an alcoholic. While we were dating, I never saw it. He was functioning, held down a job, and projected the image of the perfect man.

My husband did everything in extremes. He was extremely loving: telling me every day how much he loved me, and how he could not live without me. But then there were periods of extreme depression in which he refused to get out of bed and even threatened to kill himself, claiming I was the only reason he had to live. I had always been the savior, and here I was again, trying to hold my family together. I liked that he needed me, and that became my addiction. My purpose in life was to save him.

In the beginning, the drunken episodes were manageable. He would be falling down drunk, and I would carry him home. He would promise never to drink again, and I foolishly believed him. But then things began to get out of hand. The alcohol that he was using to mask his manic and depressive states was making everything worse, and when the alcohol could no longer medicate his moods, he was no longer able to manage his illness. He started moving into these extreme highs and lows, staying up all night doing crazy things. When I would say, "This isn't normal," he would get very defensive. He did not want me to unveil any of this. He was so good at hiding and masking his issues, and he saw me as a threat.

I had never dealt with mental illness and alcoholism, and I was feeling overwhelmed. I contacted his mother, and together we set up a meeting with a psychologist. We bamboozled him into attending the meeting, and when he got there and saw me, his mother, and the doctor sitting there, he felt betrayed by me, and things were never the same between us. To this day, I wonder if I should have done it differently.

The drinking escalated and one night he was up late drinking, lit a candle, and fell asleep. The candle got knocked over and the house caught on fire. I realized that me and my kids were in danger. My friends and family insisted that we get out of the house. As I left him, I was in a fog; a total state of shock. My heart was crying, stay, but my head was screaming, leave! As I launched out on my own again, there was such a sense of sadness. I would look out at all the pretty houses around me and wonder if I was the only one who was living a lie. I felt like such a failure, so lost and alone.

I am so thankful that I kept going to counseling; it saved me. My counselor had me reading about alcoholism and codependency. I thought I was strong enough to love him out of it, but by learning about the disease, I came to see what I contributed to the issues and what was not my fault. My counselor helped me realize that I had to focus on me, and that I could not "save" him. That is when I began

73

exploring my faith tradition, and discovered a number of self-care practices, such as Bible reading, meditation and prayer. To this day, I spend my mornings sitting with God and allowing myself to be loved unconditionally. I had spent my life defining myself through other people's eyes. But out of that terrible place of sadness, I finally started to see me: not the me that I was "supposed" to be, but the one I was born to be. I felt like I had died and had been resurrected.

> I had spent my life defining myself through other people's eyes. But out of that terrible place of sadness, I finally started to see me: not the me that I was "supposed" to be, but the one I was born to be.

A few years passed. I was in a job that I did not really like, but I was successful at it. When my company went through a restructuring and my position was eliminated, I was scared and wondered how we would make it. Had this happened prior to my coming to a place of peace in my life, it would have devastated me. However, somehow I knew that God had something better for me. I received a severance package and decided that while I was in my season of looking for employment I would dedicate myself to strengthening my relationship with God. I threw myself into the local church, into Bible studies, into reading spiritual books, and was actively seeking God's direction. I decided I did not want to go back to a nine-to-five job that did not mean anything to me other than a paycheck. I wanted to do something meaningful. I decided I wanted to make a transition out of the corporate world into the nonprofit world. As I shared with people my desire for meaningful work, I began hearing Wendy's name everywhere I went. The fifth time I heard her name, I decided to give her a call.

Deciding to join the Embrace team was a huge sacrifice financially for me, and I will be honest that even a year after joining the team I still mourn the loss of the big paycheck, the title, and the fancy office, but I would not trade what I have gained for anything. I now get paid in hugs and thank-yous, and it is amazing how far that can carry me. I also am surrounded by addicts who hold me accountable, and who challenge me to be the best me I can be. They have become some of my best friends and have helped me to see myself through new eyes. I love that I go to a job where we pray, where my gifts are valued, and where I am encouraged to share my passion with others. My favorite thing to do is to share our story. I love the story of Embrace, but I realize that there is no one story; the story of Embrace is made up of the stories of many people. It does not matter how many times I hear these stories, I always come to tears and admire the courage of those who share. Like them, I have shared my story in the hope that it too will help others move from their pit of despair to a place of peace and joy.

I am so thankful that God has taken the loss of the person who I thought was the best friend I could ever have, and has given me a whole new community of friends who love me just the way I am.

Sharon's dream: That other women trapped in relationships with addicts will find the strength to focus on their own needs.

---

10 Crazy Dreamers

The people who are living out their faith in compassion are beacons of light, illuminating the landscape around them. They are transforming our cities one person at a time, while building up civil society.

—BARBARA J. ELLIOTT

Shortly after the shooting, Stephanie's fall into addiction, and the announcement regarding the sale of the church, Aileen confided in me that she needed to step back so that she could take on an additional foster child. My little honeymoon team was slowly vanishing. Only Rosalind, Georgiana, and Brickhouse remained.

The demands of seminary, a growing ministry, and a lack of support left me overwhelmed and ready to give up. Perhaps this experiment was just that: an experiment. I had learned a lot; perhaps that was the point. I tried to convince Rosalind that it was time to let our ministry go. She refused, saying, "I don't know where I would be without Embrace, and I am not going to give up because of a little bump in the road."

Funny. Rosy saw the loss of our team and our facility, and our lack of options as a "little bump." To me these obstacles made a giant mountain!

I made a deal with her: I would put out a request for space on a local nonprofit listserver, and if God provided a space within our budget, we would keep going. I sent the e-mail just to prove to Rosalind that we had reached a dead end. I was shocked when I got two e-mails instructing me to contact Larry Lindsey who ran a nonprofit called First Contractors (www.firstcontractors.org).

The building was so nice. I almost did not go in, certain that I could not afford it. However, curiosity won out. Larry Lindsey is a handsome, soft-spoken African American gentleman. Five years prior to our meeting, he had started his own nonprofit, helping youth who were aging out of the foster-care system. These youth, all of whom lived in group homes, were at high risk for engaging in criminal activity and for becoming homeless. First Contractors taught them construction skills to help them transition into the workforce.

Larry showed me a seven-hundred-square-foot office, a large common room, and (I almost fainted when I saw) the one-thousand-square-foot warehouse, complete with a loading dock! For over a year, we had been hauling heavy furniture up and down a steep set of stairs into the Sunday-school wing of the church. I could not believe I was lusting after a loading dock, but it was the most beautiful thing I had ever seen!

I was almost in tears by the time we finished the tour; I wanted it so badly but knew we could not afford it. I asked Larry how much, and he said, "Eight hundred dollars a month." I thanked him for his time, told him we could not afford it, and turned to leave.

He said, "Wait. How about $600?" Again, I thanked him but knew I could not raise that kind of money.

He asked, "What can you afford?"

I was embarrassed to tell him $200, so I lied and said, "$350."

He smiled and said, "My board is going to kill me, but if you are willing to go up to $500 in three months, I will make it work somehow." I had no idea where I would get $350 a month let alone $500 thereafter. My board was made up of my friends who simply wanted to encourage me. None of them were giving financially at that point, and we did not even know they were supposed to be the ones to help raise money. That came as shock to us all a few years later when I took a class on board development.

When I told my board president, Karen O'Brien—the Yada Yada Karen who dreamed of taking the excess of the suburbs into the city, she immediately recognized the sacrifice that Larry was making. She and the rest of the board supported the decision to lease the building. I had gotten a $10,000 grant from Valparaiso University's "Practicing Our Faith" grant program. It was the first grant I had ever applied for, and I naively thought getting grants would be a piece of cake. It was the first and last grant of that size I would get for more than two years. However, it was just the influx of cash we needed to get the ministry off the ground.

Larry Lindsey was the first of many fellow dreamers who were crazy enough to start their own nonprofit. I think it is the hardest thing one can attempt to do. Like Larry and me, many nonprofit founders begin doing a good work because they feel called. Most do not have sophisticated business plans, funding strategies, or well-developed boards. Most are just people seeking to help other people. However, you do not survive for long without a strategy, funding, and the support of others.

I loved being in the First Contractors building because somehow in his quiet way Larry validated my call. He also gave me hope; after all, he had done it.

While I was in seminary, I heard a lot about minister burnout. I know that in the fall of 2006 I was a prime candidate for it. While the Yada Yadas were still meeting, I was not finding the level of support I needed. Most of them thought I should slow down, focus on my family, and let the ministry go until after I graduated. While that sounded good, I sensed that was not what God intended. I longed to find a group that would support me and not encourage me to turn back.

I saw a post on a list server for ministers that said, "Working with single mothers? Looking for a group to encourage you and support you in your efforts? If so, come to West End Assembly of God at 6:00 p.m. Wednesday to meet others who are serving single mothers." It was an answer to prayer. As I arrived at the gathering, I had no idea what to expect. As the women entered, each quietly took a seat. I was fidgety, wondering, "Did I belong here?" Our ministry was still very small, and we were only working with about a half dozen families a month.

At 6:00 p.m. on the dot, a beautiful woman with flowing dark hair and an animated smile entered the room. She casually plopped down across from me and said in a thick upstate-New York accent, "Does anyone else feel like they are doing this work alone?"

We all nodded in agreement.

"Do the rest of you sometimes think you are crazy for trying to help people?"

This question provoked laughter, smiles, and shouts of agreement. I instantly liked this lady. Sylvia Stewart was so real, so down-to-earth. She captured in those first two statements exactly what I was feeling.

Then she looked at us all and said, "Well, I am here tonight because I am just as crazy as you guys. I figured if the world wants to label me a nut, that I needed to find the rest of the crazies so we could all be insane together."

That night was the first meeting of what grew into The Bridge, an informal gathering of faith-based-nonprofit leaders, most of whom are founding executive directors. We gather regularly for prayer, support, and just to vent. We share resources, make referrals to one another, and keep one another in the loop about funding opportunities. The Bridge is my reality check. When I think I have lost my mind, they remind me that it is the world that has gotten off track. We are not a perfect bunch of saints; we are just a bunch of broken, crazy people seeking to live our faith in a tangible way. Everyone needs a group of peers to support and encourage them, especially those who spend their time caring for others.

> *Everyone needs a group of peers to support and encourage them, especially those who spend their time caring for others.*

Though I had lost part of my community when Aileen and Stephanie had departed the ministry, God had not abandoned me but had led me to a new community that was able to help me get to the next level.

Sylvia Stewart is the Executive Director of Fresh Start for Single Mothers (www.whatsnextfreshstart.org), and she shared with me her journey from being a stay-at-home mom to being a voice and a support-network for single mothers.

Interview with Sylvia Stewart

In 1999 I did a Beth Moore study called *Breaking Free*. In that study she asked the question, "Who do you need to forgive in your life?" I had never really thought about it, but as I prayed, I realized that I had never forgiven my high-school boyfriend. I was in a relationship with him for four years, one that was physically and emotionally abusive. As I worked through that Bible study, I said to God, "I will forgive, but you have to take it and create something good out of it."

A few days after praying that prayer, I was cooking dinner for my family, and I saw a story on television about a battered-women's shelter in a rural community about an hour from my home, that was in jeopardy of closing due to a lack of funding. I asked myself, how can I help? I am a hairdresser by trade, so I thought I could go and cut the ladies' hair. As I prepared to visit the shelter the following week, I started collecting food, toys, clothing, and other things I thought they might need. I went in bearing gifts, and the ladies opened up to me. One woman said she had not had her hair cut in ten years because her husband was so abusive that he would not allow her out of the house.

When I left there, I felt a sense of fulfillment that I had been lacking for years. I had been asking myself, why am I so dissatisfied with my life? Though I had two beautiful children, a loving husband, a nice home, and the privilege of being a stay-at-home mom, there was this emptiness inside me, like something was missing. But that night I felt full for the first time in a long time. I began getting more involved with the shelter by raising funds, and collecting donations, and even arranged to have their building renovated, complete with new furnishings.

A few years later, the board of directors instructed the executive director to remove all the faith elements of the program. The faith element was optional to all residents, but the board did not want to risk losing their funding. The director, who was also the founder of the program, refused and was terminated. I decided to discontinue my affiliation.

At that point, a group of single mothers at my church wanted to create a support group for single mothers. The women felt like they did not fit in with the singles' ministry or with the women's ministry. So Sarah Owens, a few other ladies, and I designed an eight-week program that would ultimately become the Fresh Start program. The program initially consisted of weekly workshops on topics of interest to our mothers. We offered childcare, and we shared a meal together. It was built on the Isaiah 61 concept of "beauty out of ashes."

We had women calling from all over the city wanting to participate, but our program was full. So I spent one summer writing out the curriculum and developing policies and procedures so that other congregations could run the program. Later we created a phase 2, which was more of an introspective study of the fruits of the Holy Spirit, and a phase 3 Bible study. What started out as an eight-week program is now a twenty-week program. These groups become a very important support network for our ladies, and many of them ultimately moved into leadership to help new single mothers. We currently have six programs in operation across the country and others under development in response to requests from pastors who are overseas.

We realized that we could not see the needs of these families and not try to meet them. We began making small financial grants to those women who were connected to the program toward things like past-due rent, utility bills, and car repair. We also take in a large amount of in-kind donations and redistribute those to our families. On average, we give away more than ten thousand dollars per year in financial assistance and over one hundred thousand dollars in material donations.

I take my role as a leader very seriously. I have women calling me continually, looking for help. Even if I do not have the answer, I call them back. I hear so many women complain that they call organizations, and no one ever returns their call. I want them to know that there are people who really do care. We cannot always fix the problem, but at least they know they are not alone.

I work an average of thirty hours a week as a volunteer executive director. I have a volunteer team of fourteen people who support the Fresh Start location that I lead. I have had the same core team for the past six years. Over 50 percent of our volunteers are single mothers who have gone through the program, and who want to return and help the next family.

I have been so blessed by what I do. I love that through simple acts of kindness I can make someone else's life a little easier. I have also been blessed to have all I have; it would be selfish not to be a blessing to others. You simply cannot be a Christ follower and choose to live selfishly.

When you get that right combination of a workable solution and a woman who is willing to take the necessary steps, it is so wonderful to see what God can do, to see them smile, and to hear their testimonies. That is what it is all about. We can't do it all. But we can encourage them, build their self-esteem, and share with them how God can help them overcome, forgive, and move forward.

My greatest frustration is that Christian-based nonprofits are often penalized for being Christian. Often the faith elements of Christian programs have to be watered down or removed in order to secure funding. I am not going to downplay Christ, because if it were not for my faith, I would not be doing this.

We work with a lot of women who have never been to church, and we have women from all faiths in the program. However, we do not fail to share where we have found our power. They can choose to embrace that element or not, but either way, they receive the same love, support, and encouragement as any other participant. We are there simply to welcome people in with open arms, without judgment; and that is really what I think Christians are supposed to do. We are called to meet people where they are.

One day I sent out that e-mail looking for other ministries serving single moms, I was hoping to connect with additional resources for my mothers. That original team, consisting of myself, Wendy, and Gwen Mancini, recognized that this little group, which became known as The Bridge, could provide to faith-based-nonprofit leaders what we most desperately needed: peer support. We wanted to develop a strong network in order to provide support for one another and in order to build a better system for serving our clients.

The best part of The Bridge is that I meet a lot of wonderful people, and we have built a lot of partnerships. Most of the nonprofits who attend The Bridge are small, without big marketing budgets or high-profile events; but we are all out there doing good work and helping a lot of people. I love meeting with this group because we are all in the same boat. Most of us are not paid, don't have a big staff, are all overextended; but when we get together we can stop, pray, and encourage one another to keep up the good fight. It is inspiring to hear what God is doing in these other organizations. There is such a great spirit at The Bridge meetings because we are not competing against one another; we truly want to see the other succeed.

Sylvia's dream: To expand the Fresh Start program to help provide support to more single mothers and their children.

---

11 Sacrificial Dreams

I had come to see that the great tragedy of the church is not that rich Christians do not care about the poor but that rich Christians do not know the poor . . . I truly believe that when the poor meet the rich, riches will have no meaning. And when the rich meet the poor, we will see poverty come to an end.

—SHANE CLAIBORNE

With our space issue solved, we faced another challenge: too much to do. I was in my final semester of seminary and realized I could not keep up with the enormous amount of administrative duties that accompany running a nonprofit, so we hired our first staff. There were many nights when I lost sleep worrying about paying the bills and making payroll, but somehow it always worked out.

That is pretty much how the next two years went. We just started stepping out on faith, and God began meeting our needs one at a time. Never giving us room for comfort but always supplying just what we needed right when we needed it. My team at this point consisted almost entirely of formerly homeless individuals. I would share my concerns over finances and every time be chastised for my lack of faith. Honestly, it got quite annoying. My volunteer staff seemed not to care about budgets and development plans. They just challenged me to pray and trust.

I realized that for them, faith was the only option. They had no other resources to lean on. If God did not provide, no one would. I, on the other hand, had always had resources. Even when Enron failed and we lost our income, my family and friends were there to help. My homeless friends did not have that, for their families and friends were as poor as they were. They had no one but God. I still envy their level of faith and continue to battle with simply trusting and letting go.

Before I went into the ministry, I was a CPA and spent six years as an auditor. I like the numbers to make sense. I like everything to balance and to be able to do budgets and forecasts; doing forecasts with giant negative numbers at the bottom line caused me great distress. But Embrace was not mine. It was theirs.

I first met Patricia during our early days in Highland Park. Like Rosalind, she had fled her abuser and come to Richmond not knowing anyone. She shared that she had five children, and when I tried to give her five beds, she refused, saying, "There are other families that need them more than us."

Patricia and her family were living in a poorly constructed, drafty, two-bedroom house in Highland Park. Patricia worked nights but would come and help out at Embrace before she went to work. One of her daughters had cerebral palsy. Patricia did not have a car, and her daughter had to go to physical therapy three times a week. The van service that offers rides to low-income individuals was often late, and on occasion failed to show up. This caused Patricia to miss work, consequently her employer let her go. I was sharing Patricia's challenges with one of my neighbors, Sonya, when she stopped me and asked, "Would a minivan be of any use to her?"

Patricia was in tears the day she got the keys to her very own van. That rainy day Sonya accompanied me to meet Patricia and her family. The rain was pouring down as we stood outside a local McDonald's and offered up a prayer of praise to God for this amazing gift. Each of Patricia's children contributed to the prayer, and each took their turn hugging and thanking this stranger, Sonya, who had just radically improved their lives. Patricia went on to secure not one, but two jobs now that she had dependable transportation.

One day after visiting with Patricia in her tiny house, I pulled into the driveway of my five-bedroom, 3800-square-foot home and was deeply convicted. My husband and I were giving as much as we could monthly to keep the ministry going, but it was creating a strain on our personal finances. As I sat in front of my beautiful home asking God to provide resources for the ministry so that we could help families like

Patricia's, I realized that God had provided all we needed. I had just made choices that were preventing me from using those provisions to help others. My husband had a good job and earned a nice salary, but it was all going toward the mortgage on a home that was far bigger than what we truly needed. In the meantime, a mother of five continued to live in a drafty two-bedroom home in one of the roughest neighborhoods in Richmond. Were we more deserving than Patricia and her family? Had we truly earned the right to live this way?

The disparity between the inner-city poverty and my suburban community was causing me a great amount of discomfort, and I began to resent my affluent lifestyle.

This venture into urban ministry was becoming quite personal, and honestly it was very uncomfortable. Every week some of Richmond's poorest residents would come and give all they had to keep the ministry alive while I sat in my comfortable suburban home. The disparity between the inner-city poverty and my suburban community was causing me a great amount of discomfort, and I began to resent my affluent lifestyle.

I shared my quandary with my husband, and he jokingly asked, "What do you want to do—sell the house?"

When I said yes, I thought he would seek to have me committed or insist I stop serving the poor or resent my asking him to make such a huge sacrifice. But instead he simply said, "That's fine with me."

As you have probably figured out by now, I am married to a saint. While I was in seminary and juggling the demands of being a mother, writing papers, and starting a ministry, people would ask me, how do you do all that? The truth is I didn't do any of it alone. My husband has sacrificed far more than I have so that I could do what I felt called to do. I am truly blessed to be loved by someone who is willing to do whatever it takes for me to be who I am called to be. During the darkest times, when I wanted to quit, it was my faithful husband, Chris, who would say, "You know you will not be happy unless you are doing this." He knows me better than anyone.

My family was amazing about the move. My children did not totally understand why we had to move from our wonderful home with its fabulous acre lot into a more modest home in a less-expensive community, but they took it in stride. Since our girls had been uprooted when we had moved from Texas to Virginia, we thought it best to keep them in the same schools, which meant staying in Woodlake, despite my desire to move closer to the city. The new home was a compromise that worked for everyone. The greatest thing about the move was the financial freedom we now had. Without this sacrifice, I doubt the ministry would have survived.

The sacrifice my family made is modest compared to the sacrifice made by those who were serving beside me in the city. Some were taking off work on distribution days so that they could be a part of Embrace. Others were bringing me small offerings from their limited incomes. And still others were forgoing paid employment so that the ministry could keep going. I was living the parable of the widow's mite, and I began to understand why Jesus said, "Blessed are the poor." My new friends were so willing to give of themselves and all they had, so how could I do any less?

Insights from Chris McCaig

When Wendy first shared how uncomfortable she was with where we lived, I initially felt threatened. I thought she was going to insist we move into the city in the middle of a ghetto. But when I realized what she was asking, and I convinced her it was not a good idea for us to move into the city, it was not a hard decision. It was clear we should move. For me, it is all part of the journey. That journey started back when the pastor of the first church we ever joined was trying to convince me of the value of the Christian faith. It was a real struggle for me, because I look at things through the lens of logic, and he was trying to help me grasp the concept of faith. That is what all this comes down to: faith. Without faith you have nothing. When my dad taught me to swim, I was scared to death at first, but I had to have faith that he knew best even though I thought I would die. You have to learn to have faith and just make the jump.

When I hear some Christians say, "I am saved," I wonder what they mean by that. To me, it means that I have faith that God will show me the direction I am to go as I seek to do what God would have me do. It was a leap of faith knowing that God was leading Wendy to do something that would require a sacrifice for our family. I have never had a call to work directly with the poor like Wendy does, but I do nonetheless have a strong call—a call to support Wendy in what God has called her to do. Sometimes it takes me out of my comfort zone, but it all goes back to my primary call to support Wendy. It has nothing to do with Wendy, but more my commitment to God and to do what God called me to do in supporting her. God put us together for a reason. I can't stand to see Wendy hurt, and if she wants to do something, and if it feels right, then I want to do it. Sometimes it is an immediate knowing, and other times I have to spend a good amount of time in prayer and discernment. But when she approached me about selling the house, it was just an immediate knowing. Military history teaches that success in battle has as much to do with logistics as it does with the people on the front lines. Without a good support system, you will lose. I am not called to the front lines; I am called to make sure the people on the front lines have what they need to succeed.

We were feeling the financial pressure to help support Embrace. As a family we have never really cared about what other people think. I never really felt like I belonged in the original community, and the large house never really felt like home to me. So selling the house was not really a big deal to me. I think God gave me that little bit of discomfort with that house because God was leading us to do this.

I am pretty distant from the homeless clients that Wendy knows. I could see logically the disconnect between our lifestyle and those she serves, and I know that often it is a lack of opportunity that limits what others can accomplish. But making a sacrifice for others you do not even know can be tough. We see that when we look at Jesus's encounter with the rich young ruler who walks away when Jesus challenges him to leave everything and follow him. If you have much, it is even harder for you to realize that some people have so little. It is hard for me to set aside thoughts of what we could do, what we could have if we choose to keep it all for ourselves. But there is also a kind of guilt that I feel when I find it hard to let go of all the stuff.

It's always been a challenge for me to understand poverty. I was raised thinking that if you work hard and do what is right, then all will go well, and that is what I expected everyone's worldview to be as well. Growing up, when I saw people who suffered from severe poverty, it always seemed that they were heading toward financial success. But with Wendy's clients, that just did not seem to be the case. I don't see that they are working hard in the way I defined working hard. What I learned, however, was they were not working, because they did not have the ability to get a job. I never realized all the barriers that they faced: transportation, education, addiction, felony conviction, lack of childcare, lack of stable housing, and on and on. Nothing is ever black and white. I learned you cannot judge a group of people until you truly get to know them. In getting to know Wendy's clients and hearing their stories, I have become far less judgmental. I have found that there are good people in all kinds of circumstances, and it has changed me. I am in no way the same as I was. I also look at wealthy people differently. I see how shallow, wasteful, and self absorbed the suburban lifestyle can be. I have never really wanted "stuff," and would be happy in a cave. But when we lived in that wealthy, suburban environment, I felt like I had to put on a persona and pretend to care about the house and the stuff. I did not feel I could be me.

I still have a lot of selfish needs and there is some "stuff" that I really do like, such as my computer, and football on TV. I think it is really important that people understand that we made a sacrifice that really was not that big a deal for us, but it made a huge difference in the lives of thousands of people. I know it scares people to think about sacrificing for people they do not know and whom they may think aren't working or helping themselves. I am not saying that it is bad for people to work hard, gain wealth, and enjoy the gifts that come with that. What I am saying is that everyone should give back. People think they will

People think they will be asked to make a significant sacrifice, but even small gifts of time and resources make a huge difference.

be asked to make a significant sacrifice, but even small gifts of time and resources make a huge difference.

I never would have imagined Wendy making her career out of caring for homeless people. But all this happened so incrementally, one little step at a time. What is so important to the process is to leave yourself open to grow and to continue to grow a little more and to continually listen for the call to go a little farther still. We have to be willing continually to allow ourselves to be stretched, to become uncomfortable as we take that next step. It is not always easy, but I know that God has a call on my life, and that is why I keep saying "Yes, Lord, I will go a little farther." I don't always like being made uncomfortable, but it always seems to make sense once I get to where God would have me go. None of the steps we made were large, but the cumulative effect has been unbelievable.

I now walk through Embrace and just smile. It just blows my mind what God has done. When I walk through with my big smile, I know people look at me and think, "Who is that guy?" The support folks never get the credit, and I really don't want any credit, but I think, "They have no idea what it took to get here, or how far this has come." It has been a really fun journey. I know there have been hard times, but that is just life. It has given our family purpose, and I think it has been helpful for our kids to see the world beyond suburban America.

While Wendy has wanted to walk away on occasion, I never had that desire. My goal was to help her get through those tough times, knowing that God has called us to this journey together and put us together to help one another through the hard times. I am not involved in the day-to-day operations of Embrace; I am involved as any husband should be—in supporting his wife, or as a wife should be—in supporting her husband.

Reflections from Caroline, age 11

When Mom and Dad first said we were moving, I screamed, "NOOOO!" I did not want to move, because my best friend lived down the street. I still like the old house more than this one, but I am glad my mom was able to keep doing Embrace. I have also made lots of new friends who live near our new house. I think what my mom does is really cool, and I like volunteering with my mom. I have come to see how much we have where we live, and how often we take it for granted. I remember going to Embrace and playing hide-and-seek with the kids from the inner city, and I really like getting to know kids from the city. I like playing with the little kids and helping babysit them while the moms are serving in the warehouse.

Reflection from Kristen, age 13

At first I was really sad about moving because it was a nice house and had a great backyard, but then Mom said we could get a dog if we moved, so I liked that part. Then when we moved, I met my two best friends, and now I am really happy we moved. I am really proud of my mom and what she does at Embrace. Everyone seems to know her, and it is kind of like she is famous. Serving at Embrace made me realize how really different the city is from where we live. It opened my eyes to a lot, and I like the homeless people my mom works with: they are really nice. When we first moved, I did not realize that by moving we were allowing Mom to continue doing Embrace. I think had I realized that, it would have made the move easier. I am really shy, and at the beginning I really did not like going to Embrace because it scared me. The first church was old, spooky, and it smelled. Then that day the guy shot a gun across the street, that really scared me. However, I have become more comfortable, and I actually like my mom's new building.

Reflections from Caitlin, age 15

Honestly, when my mom first started doing Embrace, I did not really appreciate it. I resented it because my mom used to make me go, and it felt like a chore. I was young and stupid, but now I see things differently. One of my favorite memories was helping plan birthday parties for homeless children. I think realizing that there were innocent children stuck in that mess was particularly powerful to me. We would just go through our old toys and take them down to them, and I could see how a simple toy meant everything to them. It changed me. I stopped wanting stuff.

I don't know if I have been shaped more by Embrace or more by simply having my mom as a mom, but I feel like I have a better outlook on life than many of the people I know. I think by going into the city, I have a better understanding of our world. Instead of feeling like the world is the size of my suburban neighborhood, I have had a chance to see a more diverse picture of Richmond. Intellectually, everyone knows that there is poverty and problems downtown, but they just keep that thought in the back of their minds. They don't really think about it. They know the situation is bad, and because they know it is bad, they think they can't do anything about it, and then they get distracted by other things. That is why there are people like my mom, to help people figure out what they can do to help.

Dreams of the McCaig family: To be faithful to God's call, whatever that may be.

---

12 Dream Stealers

Woe to those who make unjust laws, to those who issue oppressive decrees, to deprive the poor of their rights and withhold justice from the oppressed of my people, making widows their prey and robbing the fatherless.

—ISAIAH 10:1–2 (NIV)

Rosalind had been living in the house in Highland Park for six months when the doctors determined that her son had high levels of lead in his blood. Rosalind had come to Richmond to escape the abuse inflicted upon her by the father of her four children. She had hoped to give her children a better life but instead fell prey to a slumlord who not only refused to fix the problem with the lead paint but also refused to refund her housing deposit.

After spending eight months in a homeless shelter saving her money, Rosalind did not want her family to return to homelessness. One of our church partners had donated a car to Rosalind, so she could now live in the county, and her children could benefit from better schools. She began looking for alternative housing but had no money for a deposit. Rosalind was working full time, but every dime was going to pay her bills. We sent out an e-mail and asked all our supporters to be in prayer for Rosalind, and many sent small sums of money. In the end, we collected the nine hundred dollars Rosalind needed to secure housing for her family.

Rosalind is not alone. Over the years dozens of the families we have worked with have been so desperate to get out of the shelter that they have moved into substandard housing and in the end have paid a very high price. Some are faced with exorbitant utility bills because the homes are not well insulated. Since our clients are unable to pay those bills, the utilities are often turned off, the house becomes unlivable, and they are back on the street or in the shelter. Others move into communities with rampant crime and are robbed repeatedly until they flee. What appears to be an answer to prayer often turns into a nightmare for those at the bottom of the economic ladder.

> *What appears to be an answer to prayer often turns into a nightmare for those at the bottom of the economic ladder.*

Rosalind found a wonderful apartment complex where her family would be safe, but unfortunately a year after she moved, her car broke down. The transmission would cost fifteen hundred dollars to repair. The buses do not run in the county, so Rosalind faced a new dilemma: to risk losing her job or to buy a car fast. She chose the latter. Rosalind lacked the credit needed to purchase a car through a traditional dealer and found herself at a local dealer known for selling cars to anyone, regardless of their credit rating. Rosalind purchased a seven-year-old minivan with 90,000 miles on it for thirteen thousand dollars at 16 percent interest. The car had a bluebook value of seven thousand dollars, and the going interest rate was 6 percent. Once again Rosalind had fallen prey to an opportunist feeding off the misfortune of others. By the time I learned of her purchase, it was too late. This decision would handicap Rosalind and her family for the next five years as she pulled double shifts to keep her car payments up. It is incredibly expensive to be poor!

It seemed that everywhere Rosalind went, she came face-to-face with greed cleverly disguised as an answer to her prayers. However, the place that inflicts the most harm is often the local church. I went to visit a church once with Rosalind. It was a large, Pentecostal-style, predominately African American church, with a flamboyant preacher. He had the ability to whip the crowd into a frenzy of excitement, then deliver a prophetic word and convict the entire room with just one well-crafted line.

With sweat dripping from his forehead, he paced back and forth across the stage, shouting,

Friends, God desires to bless you! You just have to claim your blessing! When I pull into the carwash in my new convertible BMW, I leave my Bible on the dashboard so the young men who work there can see that God blesses those who seek to please him. God wants us to "bling" better than the drug dealers on the corner so that we are able to attract those the enemy is luring away through the promise of material wealth. It is Jesus Christ who has blessed me, and who gave me my impressive new home. I do not have to settle for less than the best, and neither do you! All you have to do is name it and claim it! If you believe in God and put your faith in him, He will bless you! The ushers will be coming through the aisles to collect our weekly offering. Don't forget friends, we show our faith in God through our willingness to sacrifice what we have so that God can give us all He has. He will multiply your gifts 10, 20, 100 fold. So dig deep, give sacrificially to the one who has sacrificed so much for you and then get ready to receive all you desire because the Lord is faithful, he will keep his promises and you will receive your blessing![1]

I had heard the term "prosperity gospel," but I had never actually heard it preached except on TV. In my affluent, mainline suburban church, this is not a message that would preach. But for some reason, it was highly effective with Rosalind and the other members of the congregation. Rosalind dug into her pocketbook and gave her last twenty dollars, then over lunch shared how tight money was for her and her family, but that she knew God would provide because she had been faithful. I wanted to scream, "God did not give your pastor his convertible BMW . . . you did!" However, I held my tongue. I did not understand this theology or the culture, and I had even had Christians say to me, "That teaching is needed for oppressed people because they need hope." I knew that the gospel should not change from church to church, but it took me years to gain the courage and understanding to speak against it. I did not want to take from Rosalind something that was helping her to persevere through difficult times, and I loved the spirit of faith that she possessed.

John Perkins, in his book *Beyond Charity*, points out the dangers of this theology, stating "The prosperity movement is heavily accepted among the poor but has done very little in terms of real community de-

---

1. This re-creation of part of an original sermon is the best my memory can do, several years after the encounter.

velopment at the grass roots level. It takes people's attention away from the problem, and if those people succeed it encourages them to remove themselves from the very people they ought to be identifying with and working among."[2]

About this time God brought a wonderful African American pastor into my life. Dr. Ellis O. Henderson has been a teacher and an encouragement to me for years. It was Ellis who helped me to gain clarity regarding this teaching, which was so rampant among those I served.

Ellis shared some of the history of the prosperity movement, which teaches that God desires material prosperity for all believers.

Insights from Dr. Ellis O. Henderson

Coming out of slavery, the black church was central to the survival and endurance of the African American community. Giving has always been a strong practice within the African American church, because it was seen as a way of taking care of those who were in need in the community. The history of the African American church demonstrates this strong commitment to serving others and a willingness to make financial sacrifices.

After the civil rights movement, the church began to decline in its influence as the fight for justice moved out of the hands of pastoral leaders and into the legal system, assuring that African Americans are able to move into mainstream society. As African Americans joined the middle class, they left predominantly African American communities. While at one time the African American pastor was the spokesperson of the community, over the last thirty to forty years this has changed as African Americans have gained public office.

In the 1980s as people of color became upwardly mobile and were experiencing a new level of financial freedom, the modern "prosperity gospel" was being birthed. By the late 1980s and 1990s, it took off. Capitalizing on the financial prosperity of the country at the time, the movement spread throughout the country with particular success within impoverished communities. As a result, capitalism was introduced into the church in unprecedented ways.

2. Perkins, *Beyond Charity*, 71.

As prosperity preachers like Kenneth Copeland and others began spreading this teaching largely through the use of television, their success resulted in a rapid spread of this prosperity teaching into local Charismatic and Pentecostal churches. The prosperity message teaches that if the people sow financially into the ministry of a church, they will receive God's anointing, and God will financially prosper them. I do not see any evidence of God promising "financial" blessings related to the giving of tithes and offerings. Most people do not read the Bible consistently. This is particularly true within the African American community, where most of the knowledge of the Bible comes through preaching on Sunday, which makes people highly vulnerable.

I don't know where we get the idea that if we give something, we should expect something in return from God. I think that idea is rooted in our culture. My grandmother taught me to give because there were others that had less than us. We were the poorest people on the block, but she always believed that if we took care of our neighbors, God would take care of us. We never got money, but we had many other spiritual, health, and relationship gifts. We should give out of obedience and a desire to help others rather than out of a desire to get something back. Prosperity teaching breeds a kind of "lotto-with-God" mindset where every time you put money into the offering plate, there is the expectation that it will "pay off." This attitude produces a sense of entitlement. People think, "God, I did my part; now you need to do your part."

> *Prosperity teaching breeds a kind of "lotto-with-God" mindset where every time you put money into the offering plate, there is the expectation that it will "pay off."*

My question is, do we see Jesus doing this? Much of the arguments that support this kind of teaching are taken out of context from the Old Testament, but we do not hear Jesus making these kinds of statements. Jesus said, "The poor you will always have with you," so why are we preaching that we are all going to be rich? Can you take the prosperity message to Haiti, to impoverished communities in Africa, to the poorest of the poor around the world? A true gospel message should be able to go around the world and should be just as true in all cultures, with all people.

While this teaching can breed a sense of affirmation and security within the African American community, I believe it is a false sense of security. God is the source of our security, not our belief in some blessing that we are owed by God. With our current economic crisis, those selling a prosperity message are finding that message a hard sell as their congregants are losing their jobs, their homes, and their faith.

I take the role of pastor very seriously. My grandmother always taught me to study the word for myself, to feed myself. I have a spiritual obligation to tell you the truth. I am not going to preach a message just to generate more money or to try to appease my members. My style is not for everyone. I will not turn cartwheels and flips for my members, but they will hear the truth.

Ellis's dream: That people would seek truth for themselves, directly from the Bible.

---

13 Dreams of Justice

The church often has been too cautious about its calling to justice, especially justice for those who have been excluded from places of privilege. We have forfeited our God-given responsibility to act on behalf of the poor.

—N. GORDON COSBY

Our new facility was located just blocks from a battered-women's shelter. I began visiting this and three other shelters once a month, telling the story of Stephanie, and inviting individuals to come along and get involved in helping their neighbors. During this time, with the help of Rosalind, we developed a little group of women, all of whom were victims of domestic violence, who would come and serve with us. Patricia would pick them up from the shelter in her donated van, and we would serve together in the morning, giving out furnishings, and then share a meal together.

All these ladies were single mothers, all of them needed to find paying jobs. But while they were in this season of transition, they were all willing to give of themselves to help the next woman in need. Every week, the ladies would line up outside my office in the afternoons, with requests for help or for prayer. Patricia needed help filling out her housing application. Toni needed help completing the paperwork for a program for the visually impaired. Keisha needed help with her resume. Katherine was having trouble with her landlord. Rita's son was in trouble at school. Nancy had just been diagnosed with HIV and needed prayer. Every Thursday, I spent hours in conversation and prayer with these ladies. Before long, I was overwhelmed and could no longer minister to my new friends in the way I desired.

Up until this point, none of my board members and few of my Quest ladies had been willing to commit to working with the families. This is partially because there was no real "program" or official volunteer position. Everything was very spontaneous. I could not predict who would come for help in any given week, nor could I know the gravity of the request in advance. All this uncertainty and lack of structure contributed to the lack of others' participation. However, I knew the success of Embrace depended on the involvement of not only my homeless friends but also my suburban neighbors. I decided to have my little group of urban ladies host a Christmas gathering with my board of directors. I knew that when my board met these ladies, they would fall in love with them, and I hoped that would be enough to motivate to become more involved.

On the night of the Christmas get-together, Phyllis opened up the evening with prayer, and a spirit of unity consumed our gathering. All my urban ladies were excellent cooks, and each one had brought her favorite dish. Then as our suburban guests enjoyed the unique assortment of delicious foods, each one of our ladies shared her story. First was Rosalind, who shared her story of triumph over an abusive partner; then Phyllis shared how God led her to learn to love white people; next Toni told how Embrace Richmond had given her a meaningful role to play despite her physical handicap; and Georgiana related how she was able to help these young moms by selecting all the kitchen items they needed. The last to talk was Maria.

I had met Maria nearly four months earlier in the battered-women's shelter. She was from Mexico, and the day I met her she spoke no English. I remembered her because she was so young and such a beautiful woman. She had two small girls, and she sat mesmerized as I shared with the residents of the shelter the story of Stephanie. I had no idea at the time that Maria did not understand a word I was saying.

When I went back the following month, there she sat in the audience again. I tried to explain to her that she had already done the orientation, but she just smiled and nodded and refused to move. What I later learned was that Maria was teaching herself English. It was not my amazing tale that drew Maria in, but her incredible desire to learn the language. In four short months, Maria achieved her goal. Her English was not perfect, but it was sufficient so that on this evening she was able to communicate her story to a room full of her peers and to our board of directors. I was shocked when she stood up to speak. Prior to that evening, I had only heard her speak short sentences, and she had never volunteered to share anything personal.

As Maria stood to share, the room grew silent as we all strained to understand her words.

> I grew up in Mexico. When I was fourteen, I met a Mexican American man who was an American citizen. At eighteen he promised to marry me, so I went with him to Texas. The marriage never happened.
>
> When I was pregnant with our first baby, he started beating me. The beatings got worse and worse. Then one day he beat me so badly that I thought he would kill me. That was five months ago. I was so scared because I didn't have papers, didn't speak English, didn't have a job, nor any money or family to help me, but I left him and went to a shelter.
>
> Last week when I went to court for custody, the judge told me that I had to come back in three months and prove I had a job to support my girls, and proof of legal-immigrant status. Unless I did this, he said he would give my girls back to my abuser. Sadly, I think this happens to many women like me.
>
> I met with an attorney, and he told me that it would take six months to a year to get my visa. All week I have been crying. I am so scared. I am thinking, maybe I should go back to my boyfriend. What will I do if I do not get my papers? I don't want to lose my girls. Can you all pray for me and for my girls?

Becky Kiraly-Qualls, who was our board's vice president, found herself in the corner of the room speaking to Maria for the rest of the evening. On the way home that evening, Becky felt God clearly directing her to help Maria. Becky had spent the past ten years as a single mother of two and had just recently remarried. She knew the challenges that Maria would face, and she knew with certainty that she was to walk alongside her as she faced them.

Becky called me the next day and told me that she wanted Maria to come live with her. Becky was a very successful optometrist, and she had a magnificent home on the lake. The bottom floor of the home was a playroom for her two sons, and she was offering to allow Maria and her two girls to live there in a converted apartment until she was able to live on her own.

In three short months, Becky helped Maria get her visa. She went to court with Maria and fought for custody of the girls, a battle that Maria eventually won. Maria and her children lived with Becky's family for eighteen months. During that time she attended English as a Second Language (ESL) classes, got her driver's license, and enrolled in cosmetology school so that she could become completely self-sufficient. She has moved out of Becky's home and is living with her two girls, working hard to make all her dreams become a reality.

While Maria's dedication and hard-working spirit were key to her success, it was Becky's forceful persistence that often tipped the scales in Maria's favor. Becky called me countless times enraged over the lack of compassion and care that Maria faced both in the social-services system and in the judicial system. Becky spent countless hours on the phone with social workers, advocates, and attorneys fighting to get them to hear Maria's case. She arranged for Maria's story to be told in the *Richmond Times Dispatch* and also successfully connected Maria to the Dreams Across America tour, where her story was televised by CBS.

About a year before Becky met Maria, our board was working on our formal mission statement. In one of the drafts that I sent out, I used the words "fight for justice" as a part of our mission statement. Micah 6:8 ("He has told you, O mortal, what is good; and what does the LORD require of you but to do justice, love kindness, and to walk humbly with your God" [NRSV]) had become a key verse for us, and I wanted our mission statement to reflect this commitment to go beyond charity and to embrace justice. Becky sent me back an e-mail stating that these words were too political, and that we should focus on ministering to people, not on fighting for justice. I conceded, and we removed those words form the mission statement.

I will never forget one particularly fun conversation I had with Becky. She had grown incredibly irritated by the lack of action on the part of Maria's social worker and called me to say, "It is so unjust!"

I then asked her, "So, do you think we need to fight for justice?" While the majority of the clients that I have worked with are homeless as the result of their own choices, poor money management, and addiction, some—like Maria, Rosalind, and Patricia—are simply victims.

During my last semester in seminary, I took an urban missions trip to Camden, New Jersey, and stayed at the Romero Center. The director of Social Justice Ministries, Larry DiPaul, made remarks to this effect: There are two feet to Christian social teaching. The first is charity and the second is justice. Charity says, "That man is hungry," and gives him food. Justice asks, "Why is that man hungry?" and then seeks to empower him never to be hungry again.

Reflections from Dr. Becky Kiraly-Qualls

When Wendy wanted to make part of the Embrace mission statement "fighting for justice," I said, "I don't really think that is what we are about." In the past few years, God has shown me fighting for justice is an important role Christians can play

> *God has shown me fighting for justice is an important role Christians can play in helping those trapped in poverty.*

in helping those trapped in poverty. I recently read a quotation by Edmund Burke that said, "The only thing necessary for the triumph of evil is for good men to do nothing." I have come to see the truth of this statement, initially through my relationship with Maria, and most recently with LaKisha.

I had been LaKisha's "encourager" (mentor) for about two years when she called me up and shared that she had lost her job. She was working for a nursing home that had been shut down due to health-code violations. The organization who managed her housing was about to evict her. LaKisha had found another job but was out of work for about a month and was waiting on her first paycheck. She also had several thousand dollars coming from a tax refund, so I knew that this was just a short-term need. I offered to loan her the money, but it took weeks and several phone calls to the agency before I was finally able to reach the director and stop the eviction. I feel certain that had I not advocated for LaKisha, she and her two boys would have literally been out on the street even though within a few weeks she would have had plenty of money to pay her rent.

I thought LaKisha was home free after this incident, but the next trial she faced was by far more significant. Years before, LaKisha had been sexually harassed by a co-worker. The co-worker followed her home one day, attacked her, and tried to rape her. She fought back. Fortunately, a neighbor heard her screams and called the police. The perpetrator was prosecuted. LaKisha was so traumatized by the incident that she had to go on medications and seek counseling to deal with the memories of the attack.

Now, as LaKisha settled into her new position, a senior staff member began making sexually charged statements to her, saying things like, "When I drink, it makes me horny, and I just might take you in a room, lock the door, and do some nasty things to you." LaKisha stood up to him, saying, "Don't you ever talk to me like that again!" Not only did his statement bring back memories of her being attacked, but it was highly insulting. Within a few weeks, this same man fired her without cause.

LaKisha was not the only staff member who had fallen prey to this man. He told another woman, "I was having wet dreams about you last night." He then went on to describe all the vulgar things he dreamed of doing to her. When I heard about the things he had said to both LaKisha and her friend, I decided to have a conversation with the director of the organization. She seemed very nice and caring, but she refused to believe LaKisha. I assured her that there were others who had been harassed by this man. She said she did not believe the allegations unless others would come forward. I told her "That is very risky for these ladies since this man is in a position to fire them." She assured me that if others came forward, they would be protected.

We assured LaKisha's friend that it would be safe, so that same day she told the director what had been happening. That was on a Friday. When she reported for work the following Monday, she was told that she had been suspended because she was under investigation. The next day she was fired. I felt just terrible! I was so mad that I decided to lodge a complaint at the corporate level of the organization, not only to protect the nurses like LaKisha and her friend, but also to protect the residents of the nursing home. The only response we ever got from corporate was, "She is still fired." We learned that corporate did investigate the claims but never called LaKisha or the other woman who was fired to get the full story. Of course, none of the other women who were still working at the organization would talk about what was going on, because they had seen what happened to LaKisha and her friend. We decided to move on with our lives. LaKisha and her friend both found new jobs within a week, so we just let it go.

In June, LaKisha and her friend both got calls from the nursing board informing them that their previous employer had filed a report claiming that they were terminated for using inappropriate language and combative behaviors with the staff and residence. LaKisha had been warned that this administration had a well-established pattern of turning in to the nursing board any women who crossed them. The report to the nursing board was filed within days of the corporate investigation.

I went with LaKisha to the nursing board's interrogation. I pointed out to the investigator that these ladies had been allowed no voice: "Those who are still there are not willing to sign a statement, because if they sign it, they will get fired; and worse, they will be turned into the nursing board on fraudulent charges."

The nursing board agreed that we could bring in women to validate what was going on while keeping their identities anonymous. Once the women realized what was at stake—that LaKisha and her friend were at risk of losing their licenses and their livelihood—they found the courage to speak. The most convicting testimony was from a woman who had been having sex in the parking lot with the man who had sexually harassed LaKisha and her friend. When she said that she did not want to have sex with him anymore because she felt that it was wrong, he threatened to suspend her. One woman informed them that he had pulled out his private parts and had started masturbating in front of her. We also found out that there were prior complaints by nursing staff against this man at the nursing home where he had formerly worked. The nursing board concluded that there was insufficient evidence against LaKisha and her friend, and the case was closed.

While we are thankful that LaKisha was cleared, it is scary that the man is still in the same position. We were going to walk away, but now that the extent of the abuse was known, we fought to have him terminated. I know LaKisha and her friend and the other women never would have stood up for themselves had I not encouraged them. What was terrifying to me was that he was in a position of authority in a nursing home, where the residents are vulnerable and may not be lucid. This fight was not just to set right what they did to LaKisha, but it was to show other women that they do have rights and a voice, and to encourage them to protect themselves from being abused.

The challenging thing is to help these women who have been so beaten down and disappointed to develop a new attitude. They have been hurt so much that they expect to be taken advantage of. As an encourager (mentor), I speak into this mindset and refocus them on God's perspective, encouraging them to always look to God to provide emotionally and financially.

Reflections from LaKisha

When all these things started happening to me, I was not sure what to do. I told Mrs. Becky about the prior abuse, and how the man's comments made me feel, because I knew she would understand. I decided I was not going to tolerate that kind of insult from any man. Mrs. Becky has taught me that I have to stand up for myself.

In the black community, girls get used to men saying inappropriate things to them and doing things to them. We just lie down and take it. So many girls think this is just how it is. I walk into grocery stores and have men say to me, "I wonder what it is like to have your legs wrapped around me," or comment on how big my breasts are. They even tell me to turn around so they can see my butt. It happens all the time! One guy was staring at me, and I said, "What are you staring at?"

He said "I ain't never done it with a girl as tall as you."

What did he think I was going to do—drop on the floor and just let him do it right there?!

I used to let people say things like that to me, but I don't any more. I now demand respect. It took me a while to get to the point where I would stand up to men. I did it the first time as an experiment. Then as I gained confidence, I became bolder. When I was a girl, I thought if the boy said he loved me, it was OK to have sex with him. But I now want more. Mrs. Becky taught me that, too.

I used to be afraid of being by myself. I was in an abusive relationship for years and used to say, "I love him; he is everything to me." Then he would beat the crap out of me. I thought I could not live without him. He would say, "I'm sorry. I have changed." I believed him. I even took him back twice, and every time, the violence got worse. I realized that I didn't want my sons to see me going through that. I don't ever want them to think that is how you treat a woman.

I finally said, "I have had enough!" That was two years ago, and I am standing firm. Last week Mrs. Becky and I were on our way to Wal-Mart. Two men came on to me and were looking for a relationship with me right in front of her. I gave them my favorite line, "I don't have a man, because I don't want a man. I'm waiting on God to bring me my 'God-man.'" I can now be alone. I can even be happy by myself. I came to realize that I have a man. His name is Jesus, and he is all I need.

I love Mrs. Becky to death, because I can be having a bad day and I know she will listen to me without judging me or throwing my past in my face. I can't go to my family when I need a shoulder to cry on or need someone to say, "You are doing good." I don't get that kind of encouragement from my family. I turn to Mrs. Becky because I know she is going to give me the right answer, and say, "Way to go, LaKisha," or, "Go, God!"

I hope other African American women will see the benefit of having an encourager. It took a while for me to learn to trust Mrs. Becky, because I had been disappointed and let down by so many people. In the beginning she called me every day, sometimes two and three times a day. At first I thought, "She's on something!" because she was always so upbeat and so full of energy. But her excitement has rubbed off on me. I get up in the morning excited and wondering, "What is God going to do today?" I know he is going to do something good. Mrs. Becky does not always have the answers, but she always says, "Well, let's pray about it." She is teaching me to give God more of the credit. I have really focused on growing my relationship with God. I grew up in the church, but I stayed away. People see where I have been and where I am now. I assure them that I did not get here on my own. Trust and believe: It was all God.

Becky's dream: That more Christians would become encouragers and fight for justice.

LaKisha's dream: To give back to the community by helping others.

14 Entitled to Dream

I know only too well how a program that should be a safety net is actually discouraging initiative, rewarding dependency, and reinforcing racism for both blacks and whites.

—JOHN PERKINS

Early on in our ministry, we began getting calls from suburban youth groups who wanted to serve in the inner city. Our ministry was a perfect fit for youth groups because of the high demand for unskilled labor needed to sort and organize donations. Over the years we expanded our service options and were working with a large suburban youth group assisting an inner-city elementary school with a cleaning project. Four local youth aged ten to fourteen walked up and said, "We want to volunteer. Can we help?" The school was not comfortable with the young men helping inside the building, because there was no parental consent, so I asked them to help me load a few items into my car.

Not two minutes into their "serving" they asked, "So how much are you going to pay us for helping you?"

I was shocked. I had experienced this kind of "helping" in so-called Third-World countries but never so blatantly in a First-World urban setting.

I said, "I don't have any money."

The ringleader offered, "You can give us all a soda."

I said, "I don't have any soda."

Then the littlest one asked, "Can you give us a cold glass of water?"

I agreed to give them all a glass of water, but they would have to come to my building down the street. That was obviously not the answer they wanted, so their "service" ended before we reached my car.

When we started giving away furniture, I thought we were unique. I later learned that there are more than fifty furniture banks across the country. Whereas I never saw Embrace as a furniture bank but instead as a ministry that gave away furniture, the rest of the community began to identify us exclusively with furniture, and word began to spread. We were getting requests from case managers and shelters all over the city to help their clients. I realized I could no longer go and visit with clients in all the shelters, so we solicited the advice of the National Furniture Bank Association (www.help1up.org) and learned that most of the furniture banks worked through referrals, and that many used a voucher system. Referral partners were screened by the furniture banks, and then the referral partners screened their clients. The referral partners also purchased vouchers for a nominal price—fifteen dollars when we began the program—and gave those vouchers to their clients, who scheduled an appointment. This process accomplished two goals: 1) it saved us time, because all the clients came to us prequalified, and the case managers completed all the paperwork; but, 2), it also generated a small amount of revenue.

Unfortunately, there was a downside to creating a formal "program." In the beginning, we were just a bunch of people trying to help our neighbors. Everything was free, and if we did not have a particular item, no one complained; they just appreciated what they could get. I personally met with each client and told him or her how we had started the ministry because a homeless woman wanted to give back, and I invited each client to join our team. Prior to starting the voucher system, roughly 30 percent of those we served came and served alongside us at least once; many stayed for years. When we instituted the voucher system, we came face-to-face with a new spirit, a spirit that anyone working in social services knows all too well: the spirit of entitlement. People began asking, "Do we have to serve to get furniture?" The answer was always no, but that question never arose prior to the voucher system. When we would say, "No, it is your choice," I would see people snicker and roll their eyes as if to say, "Yeah, well you ain't never going to see me work for nothing."

As people shopped, we began to hear, "My case manager said I could get four beds, so why are you telling me I can only get two? What do you mean you don't have a dresser? I have to have a dresser!"

While these more challenging people were not the norm, just one or two shoppers with this attitude was enough to run off even the most seasoned volunteer. We saw our volunteer numbers drop steadily over the next year, and fewer and fewer of those we were serving were offering to help the next family in need. In our attempt to streamline our process and make things more efficient, we unknowingly institutionalized Embrace and robbed our efforts of the spirit that made it so beautiful. We were no longer a ministry with a furniture bank; we were a furniture bank that used to be a ministry.

The spirit of entitlement is rampant among individuals who have been at the bottom of the economic ladder. Anytime we create the idea that someone deserves assistance, we are breeding a spirit of entitlement. I saw this in my own children when we started giving them an allowance: in the beginning they were grateful, but they quickly began to argue that they "deserved more." At the first sign of my children's taking on this attitude, we eliminated "allowances" and created "paying chores," and the spirit of entitlement vanished. Ruby K. Payne, Philip E. DeVol, and Terie Dreussi Smith, in their insightful book called *Bridges Out of Poverty*, illustrate the impact of entitlements in the cycle of generational poverty: "Generational poverty has its own culture, hidden rules, and belief systems. One of the key indicators of whether it is generational or situational poverty is the prevailing attitude. Often the attitude in generational poverty is that society owes one a living. In situational poverty the attitude is often one of pride and a refusal to accept charity."[1]

In the beginning I used to pray, "God, help me separate the goats from the sheep." I knew that some people were simply not ready to be a part of what we were about, and that trying to minister to everyone, especially those with an attitude of entitlement, would require more resources than we had. As I studied Matthew 25:31–46, I found the key to identifying the sheep: sheep serve others. The power behind our ministry was always in serving together side by side; that was where authentic relationships were formed. It is those authentic relationships that trans-

---

1. Payne, et al. *Bridges Out of Poverty*, 65.

formed the lives of all who served, both rich and poor. I was not willing to allow this aspect of our ministry to die.

We decided to institute a volunteer-incentive program, according to which those who served would receive points, which they could redeem in the furniture bank. We continued to give away furniture at the same rate we always had, but those who returned to help others received additional assistance. While the programmatic nature of the plan still bred a level of entitlement, we saw this spirit dissipate as relationships formed, and people began to serve because they liked being a part of the team, and not solely because they wanted the stuff. It is not a perfect system, but it is the best solution we have found. It offers people dignity and pride while recognizing that they have a valuable contribution to make.

The welfare system and public-housing authorities have also instituted their own community-service requirements. If you live in public housing or receive Temporary Assistance for Needy Families (TANF) and are not working, you have to do "community service." Recently I was visiting a family in one of the public-housing projects and heard a woman say, "I wish I had someplace to go during the day. It is so hot in my apartment."

I offered, "You could come join one of our community-service teams."

With a disgusted look she said, "I don't have to do community service!"

I had unknowingly insulted her. In her mind the only people who do community service are those who are "required" to serve either by the judicial system or by social services. We have turned serving our neighbors into a form of punishment! It seems that every attempt we make at "mandating" right behavior only undermines the very thing we are trying to instill.

It seems that every attempt we make at "mandating" right behavior only undermines the very thing we are trying to instill.

Throughout the years a number of individuals have elected to go against the culture of getting, and instead give. These urban "street saints" have restored my faith in what God had called us to do by asking people to join our team. The first to join our team was Mrs. Georgiana. I asked her to share why she was so committed to service and to reflect upon why so few others have been willing to make a similar commitment.

The second urban servant who impressed me through her service to others was Rosalind. Unlike Georgiana, Rosalind was raised in poverty in the projects in New York and for years lived her life trapped in hopelessness. Rosalind is rare. She has escaped generational poverty, and her children will, I hope, never know the sense of utter hopelessness that she experienced.

Interview with Georgiana

I am seventy-six years old. I have twelve children and forty-two grandchildren. I have been through a lot and seen a lot, and I hope I will see a lot more before I go. I am originally from Oxford, North Carolina, and moved to Richmond about five years ago.

At seventy-six, I should have known what depression was, but I did not know what depression was 'cause I had never gone through it. I asked my neighbor, "What is depression?" and she told me. And I thought, well, maybe that is what is wrong with me. When I get depressed, I do one of two things: I either eat or I shop. I end up at J. C. Penny or Wal-Mart and in debt, or I eat all the time and gain weight. I talked to the doctor about it, and he said, "You need to find something you enjoy doing."

So I went to the senior-citizen building, and I have to tell you those people got on my nerves. My brain is not ready for that yet. I am not to the point that I want to sit around with a bunch of old people, complaining. I don't even want to hear it. They do bingo and dominos and stuff like that. Maybe I will get there one day, but I have not got there yet. I enjoy doing stuff.

I first heard about Embrace from my daughter because Embrace helped her. She encouraged me to volunteer. I remember coming to Embrace back when Wendy first started giving away furniture. She would just throw the doors open and tell folks to take what they needed, and it was wild. It was crowded in that old church, and some of the ladies that worked with me were really nice; but some of the ladies who came to get stuff were really rude. Some days were really good, and some days were really bad. Some people took what they needed, and others just took everything they could get. That was how they were raised: they were raised to take.

I have been working in the kitchen area for almost five years, and Wendy told us, if you would not want to use it, don't give it to nobody else either. So that is what I do: I put the good stuff out for our clients and I throw out the stuff I would not want in my house. We have nice stuff for people. I tell everyone about Embrace. It is a fantastic thing.

I enjoy working; sitting around is boring to me. People here are good company; everyone treats everyone right. No one is on top; we are all equal. If someone brings in some food, everyone gathers around and shares a meal. I miss those days in Highland Park when we used to eat fried chicken and share dishes that we brought in. We had a good team, and we stayed prayed up. The Bible says where two or three are gathered, Jesus is there. You have to have the Lord in everything. I want to have the right attitude with the people I work with, so I read my Bible before I come up in here. After serving here all day, I am tired, I go home, I eat, I watch TV, I read my Bible, and I sleep. I work on my soul and I try to keep a good attitude and it has helped me with the depression.

I have lived in public housing for five years. I say hi to my neighbors, and I have given them some of the furniture Embrace has given me, but I do not really know those people. If I can help, I do. That is how I was raised, and every time I have blessed others, Embrace has blessed me.

I see so many of my neighbors just sitting around, not working, not doing nothing, not willing to come to Embrace and help. I think it is laziness. People have not been taught to serve others. If you have not been taught something, you will not do it. They have the idea that if they are going to "work," then they have to get a paycheck. But I see them take jobs, and then they mess up on that. Once they been there a couple of weeks, they say, "I don't feel like going to work." Then they get fired and get mad because they can't find a job.

When my kids were young, I washed toilets, and I earned an honest paycheck. I tell them "If you can't get the job you want, work a job you need until you can get the one you want. Don't be high minded." I told my children, "You want to be a secretary, but you might have to clean that white person's toilet until you get that secretary job." You know what? I made good money cleaning houses: forty-five dollars a day!

I think some of the laziness has to do with the government payments. If people work, their rent goes up, they lose their food stamps, and their benefits get cut. I had twelve children and was a single mom, and I never took welfare. To a lot of people that government check is a paycheck. A lot of people have never worked in their life. Once people work and earn their own money, they will not be satisfied with welfare.

I am from the old school. We were taught to work hard. I think it is all in what you are taught. My grandmamma raised me, and she taught me, you don't get something for nothing. She taught me that in order for us to have vegetables in the garden, we had to go out and plant the seed and pull the weeds and water the plants. If we did not do the hard work, we did not get the vegetables. She taught me to pay my bills first, and pleasure came later. But if you don't have that, if you don't have someone teaching you, then you don't learn that. In life, you get what you put into it, and if you do not put anything into it, it is downhill all the way. I see people just sitting around, and it is pitiful. I want to help them, but their attitude is what keeps me away.

Interview with Rosalind

I grew up in Far Rockaway Park, a public-housing project in Queens, New York. I was raised by my mom; she raised five of us kids on her own. We all had different fathers. I never really knew my father, but I got to see the fathers of my brothers and sisters, and how they were with them. We really did not see mom much because she was out trying to find work or working, cleaning houses, making next to nothing. As I child, I knew what hunger was; many nights, I went to bed hungry. Mom just could not make enough to support five children. It was really hard for her.

I saw a lot growing up in the projects: abuse, neglect, and violence in the streets. I always knew it should not be that way, but it was all I had ever seen. I became very angry as a child because I knew there was better out there, but I did not know where better was. Growing up I only had one doll baby and hand-me-down clothing, and I remember being teased at school. The place where we lived had an old pool that was abandoned and fenced off because it was full of nasty water, leaches, and stuff. As children we used to go exploring around that abandoned pool. My cousin nearly drowned in that nasty pool.

When I was six years old, I had a friend named Adrian. Mom did not let me play outside much, but I remember one day Santa Claus came to give toys to the kids. So my sister took me. Then she let me and Adrian play in the courtyard while she went to play basketball. The man who played Santa Claus came up and told me and Adrian that his dog had puppies and asked if we wanted to see his puppies. Of course, we were kids; we wanted to see the puppies. My sister had told me to stay in the courtyard, but I followed the man and Adrian into the building.

Someone must have told my sister that I had gone into the building. Adrian was past the stairwell door following the man, when my sister burst through the stairwell door and found me. She dragged me from the building. I thank God that she was there. Unfortunately Adrian continued up the stairs. I learned what happened next from the newspaper. Adrian was raped and murdered by the man. He cut her body up and hid it between the buildings. At first, I did not understand what happened to Adrian. I kept looking for her, thinking I would see my friend again. The police came to our house and I told them about the man and the puppy. The police found Adrian's body and caught the man.

My mom told me growing up that my father was not a nice man. So I come from a line of abusive, dysfunctional relationships. It seemed that everyone growing up was just trying to find a way out of there. My two older sisters left home, and that made me the oldest child in the home. My mom tried to shelter us, but you cannot shelter kids from the violence and drugs of the New York City schools. I have two little brothers, and I knew I had to protect them. I knew if I became a bad ass, smoking reefer, fighting, and acting tough, people would leave us alone. So that is what I did. I earned my stripes by being the pickup girl for the drug runs, I got to know the drug dealers, beat up other girls so they all knew I was not playing, so don't mess with me. People began to look at me and say, "That chick is sixty-forty," meaning I was crazy.

When I got old enough to see there was another part of New York and was old enough to travel alone, I basically ran away by signing myself up for Job Corps, forging my mother's consent. But I realized that I missed my family, and Job Corps was kind of spooky to me. Kids would go on drug runs and never come back, and the kids would make up stories about them disappearing. Then two girls went on a trip to a strange church where they saw a séance, and someone on campus decided to practice it, I saw it and freaked out, and I left and went home.

Once I was home, I got hooked up with the wrong people again. At that time, my mother had become a functioning alcoholic, and I was dealing with a lot of things that were just too heavy for me. From the time I was ten to when I turned eleven, I was sexually molested by the cousin of one of my mother's boyfriends. I felt trapped. I had nothing. I did not want to live, and I had no one to talk to. I began questioning life. Why am I here? Who am I? Why did my mother give birth to me? I had never been to church, but I began to realize there was a supernatural realm, and God brought people into my life who did go to church, so I went with them for a while.

Then on my nineteenth birthday I was pregnant with my first child, and I could not smoke weed, or drink or party, so I decided to go to church on my birthday. We got on the bus that took us to this huge Pentecostal church. The energy in that church made me so happy. The preacher spoke about forgiveness and abuse, and it touched me, and I began crying. This really old lady said to me, "You know, darling, you are not here by accident." Then she gave me this hug, and I just held onto her and began bawling like a baby. As I was crying, she was saying things like, "God loves you," and things I had never heard before. Before she left, she told me to read Proverbs 3:5: "Trust in the LORD with all your heart and lean not on your own understanding; in all your ways acknowledge him, and he will make your paths straight" [NIV]. I stood on that Scripture for the next twenty years.

I had lots of questions about the spiritual realm, but my mom could not help me. Her parents had not taught her, and she could not teach me. I started having all kinds of trials, and there was no one who could help me. I felt so trapped. I was so angry with God. The babies, the beatings; then everyone I knew was dying. It was just all too much.

Then one weekend I stayed with the sister of my baby's daddy. She was a true Christian. For her it was not about religion, but she had a true relationship with Jesus. When I was there with her, I felt safe, because I did not think my boyfriend would abuse me in his sister's home. She did so much for me. Just being around her, being in her home, seeing her character, seeing her pray and praise. I made a commitment to join a church. Then eleven years ago, I got saved. I gave up the cocaine, the cigarettes, and the partying. To my surprise, the abuse got worse. I had used the cocaine to ease my pain, but when I gave up the drugs, I had nothing to ease my pain. I left my abuser several times, but he always found me. But this last time, I knew it was the last.

When I got out of the shelter in Richmond, I was so excited about the move, I forgot about the furniture. I was just grateful to be in my own place with my children. When I got to Embrace, I met all these women who I could see were overwhelmed with joy in serving people. I could tell they were just getting started, and, boy, oh boy, they looked like they needed more hands. I immediately knew I was coming back to service with them just to show my appreciation. I served at Embrace to save my life and to try to encourage others to save theirs. I know Embrace's doors were open to all kinds of people who were broken and hopeless. I wanted to be a mouthpiece for God. I needed to let those people see the God in me and to see how much they were loved. Embrace was the best blessing. God had planned it out for me. Embrace allowed me to operate out of the gift God gave me. I learned so much from the people I met at Embrace. In return I gave them a testimony that gave them hope for the next day.

So many people are in bondage, they want something for nothing, or they are trapped in their addictions. People who do nothing want nothing in life, because it's too much work. They are lazy, and some are from dysfunctional homes and environments, with too many excuses for why they can't. Some do only what they know, the things their parents taught them. It's sad but true. They don't just sit in their apartments alone doing nothing. Depression defeats them and sits right next to them.

When I got to Richmond, I was walking with God, and for the first time I felt free of all that bondage. While in Richmond, it seemed that every six months something would hit me like a truck out of nowhere and threaten me and my family. However, I had met Wendy and was serving at Embrace, and I found a church that taught me the truth about God and how much God loves me. Through Embrace and my church I learned to receive the good things that God had for me. I learned that I had to have a relationship with Jesus. I was broken, I needed confidence, I needed to believe in myself, and when I learned to accept the love of God, I learned how to enter into healthy relationships. Today I am happily married. God gave me a new heart, and my only desire is to serve God. I have a nice car, a nice home, and lots of material blessings, but my journey is not about the material freedom I now have; it is about the spiritual power that can never be taken from me.

> *My journey is not about the material freedom I now have; it is about the spiritual power that can never be taken from me.*

Georgiana's Dream: That people would come to know the value of hard work, and learn to serve others.

Rosalind's Dream: To help other women who feel trapped discover the power of God that can set them free no matter what their past or present circumstances may be.

---

15 Dreams of Hope

After a lifetime of exclusion, exploitation, suffering, and want, they no longer see themselves as people created in God's image with creativity, potential, and worth. They have lost the last thing that can be taken from them—hope.

—RICHARD STEARNS

Have you ever felt your heart stop at hearing the words, I love you? Those words that should bring us a sense of joy and comfort can also cause us to stop breathing when they are followed by the word goodbye. Twice in my life I have heard those words spoken as a final goodbye from two people I loved. The first time I received a call of this nature was in the fall of 1997. The following day my father took his own life: it is this loss that knocked me off that hamster wheel and made me question the meaning of our existence.

My dad was very loving, but he never said, I love you. That night when he said goodbye, as he shared with me how proud he was of me and asked me what I thought my future would hold, I could tell something was different. However, I never dreamed this would be my last conversation with him. I have replayed it in my mind a million times, looking for the answer to the question, why?

The eldest son of a second-generation German-immigrant family, my father became the man of the house at the age of thirteen when his father died of a brain aneurism. His mother was disabled and unable to work outside the home, so he went to work at a local drive-in as a carhop, moving up to fry cook, then manager, and eventually to part-owner. Over time he went from abject poverty to wealth; he lived the American Dream. I would not describe my dad as ambitious, just hard working. He loved to say, "A penny saved is a penny earned," and "You get what you work for." He instilled in me at an early age a strong work ethic.

My mom dropped out of high school and married my father at age sixteen. At age twenty-eight she got her GED and began her climb through the ranks of corporate America. Eventually she started, built, and sold her own mortgage company. Since then she has started and built numerous businesses, from an emu farm to an embroidery company. As a result of my parents' climb out of poverty, which ultimately resulted in a fair amount of wealth, I got to live that American Dream through them, and I inherited their entrepreneurial spirit.

In November 1997, however, our American Dream turned into a nightmare when my father pulled that trigger. The night before my father's funeral, I sat beseeching God to explain, why! My dad was one of the most respected men in our small community, and by far one of the most successful by worldly standards. His death made no sense to anyone. The week prior to his death, my father was diagnosed as clinically depressed and was urged to enter the hospital. After he refused, his primary-care doctor put him on an antidepressant, and four days later he was dead. It was later found that that the antidepressant that he was prescribed increased the risk of suicide, and it was taken off the market. What led to his depression? We will never know. He had a loving family and material wealth, and ran a successful business.

As I cried out to God for answers, God was silent. In anger, I opened my Bible and demanded that God speak. A friend of the family had suggested that I meditate on Romans 8:28: "And we know that in all things God works for the good of those who love him, who have been called according to his purpose" (NIV); this only elevated my level of anger. How could good come from something like this? Not even God could bring good from this tragic death. As I continued to read, I discovered one small ray of hope in Romans 9:38: "For I am convinced that neither death, nor life, nor angels, nor rulers, nor things present, nor things to come, nor powers, nor height nor depth, not anything else in all creation, will be able to separate us from the love of God in Christ Jesus our Lord."

Tears began to stream down my face as I felt God lifting me out of my own pain and assuring me that nothing could separate my father from the Creator's love. It is Romans 9:38 that I had engraved on my father's footstone, and it is that message of grace that compelled me to speak at my father's funeral. I could not explain why he had taken his life, but I could offer assurances of God's grace and mercy.

In that long, dark night before my father's funeral, I felt God's presence enveloping me as I composed a message of hope and grace that I would share the next day before hundreds of grieving friends and family members. It was during this time of prayer that I clearly felt God saying to me, "You will bring hope to the hopeless." I did not understand those words, but the impression they had on me was so strong that I shared the experience with my husband, though I am certain he thought I was crazy. It was this loss that awakened me to my senseless seeking for material success and launched me on a new journey. My parents had journeyed from poverty to prosperity, and yet depression had consumed my father. It was in my own pit of despair and grief that I discovered a pathway to a place of joy that I never would have found had I not been wounded so deeply.

Ten years later, I finally understood the prophetic words I had heard that night as I found myself surrounded by hurting, hopeless people and came face-to-face with suicide once again. It was 10:00 a.m. on July 3, 2007, when I saw Shelly's name come across my cell phone and decided to call her when I got into the office. Shelly was a former client whom I had hired to help around the office. Ten minutes later, as I listened to her voice-mail message, I knew I had made a tragic mistake. In the three years I had known her, she had rarely cried. Despite the tragedies of losing everything from her children to her home to her freedom because of her drug addiction, somehow she had held herself together. But her phone message revealed something was terribly wrong as she sobbed, "Oh Wendy, I just need to talk to someone." There was a long pause as she tried to find words and then those terrifying words, "I love you . . . Goodbye."

She swallowed a bottle of painkillers in search of relief. She just wanted to go to sleep and never wake up. She had been fighting the good fight, holding down two jobs, working seven days a week, and was starting to believe in herself again. How could she just give up after all she had gone through? Why now? Why this way? Why didn't I see this coming? Why?

I began calling her cell phone over and over again. I was about to leave the office and go in search of her when my phone rang. I breathed a sigh of relief when I saw her number but then she confirmed my worst fear. In a groggy voice she whispered, "Wendy, I did something stupid. I swallowed a bunch of pills. Can you come help me?"

My co-worker drove like a maniac down the crowded street to Shelly's apartment, as I tried to keep her talking. "Shelly, what did you take?" Shelly, the ambulance has been called. Shelly, don't go to sleep . . . Keep talking to me." As we burst into her backdoor, she was standing in the kitchen, barefoot and glassy eyed. The ambulance was nowhere in sight, so we rushed her to the emergency room where we were instructed to "Have a seat." I looked at the emergency-room nurse in total shock as though she should have known that my friend had tried to kill herself. I then mouthed the words, "She overdosed on these," and held up an empty bottle of pain pills. I could not speak those words out loud. I felt like I would offend Shelly if I shared that she had tried to kill herself. I quickly learned that this could not be our little secret: she was asked no less than two dozen times why she was there as we progressed through the maze of doctors and nurses.

After being admitted, she was given a not-so-yummy charcoal shake to drink. Better to drink charcoal than have a tube shoved down your throat. She was then pumped full of fluids, and then we waited as she continued to move in and out of consciousness. Four hours later, she seemed to be getting better. A social worker came to evaluate her, asking, "Do you think you want to go for a psychiatric evaluation?"

I wanted to scream "Duh!"

A tear trickled down Shelly's cheek, and she said in the voice of a five-year-old, frightened child "Do I have to?" directing her question first to the social worker, then to me. Knowing that Shelly had spent much of her adult life in and out of jail, I could understand her fear of being locked in a psychiatric ward, but the woman had just attempted to kill herself. I urged her to admit herself.

In the next few hours as we waited for her transfer "upstairs" to the "loony bin," as Shelly called it, I realized that her fear of the psych ward was stemming not only from a fear of being locked up but from a fear of being labeled crazy. When she was not swallowing painkillers or pumping heroin into her veins, Shelly was one of the sanest people I knew, but there was no denying that she was emotionally unstable. Who wouldn't be, after having gone through the abuse that she had endured in her short thirty-five years on this earth? Drugs had been her escape, and navigating life clean and sober proved to be an impossible task. I struggled to find the right words to comfort her, feeling completely ill equipped for the task, fearful that I would say something that would further cause her pain. I realized how far in over my head I was.

I recently watched the movie *Entertaining Angels: The Dorothy Day Story*. I expected Dorothy Day, the founder of the Catholic Worker Movement, to be some super-spiritual powerhouse who somehow avoided the pitfalls of ministry that I seemed prone to falling into, someone who made all the right choices and had all the right words. What I saw, however, was an ordinary woman who persevered despite the pain and disappointment that are inevitably a part of ministry. The movie captures vividly the pain of her failure in the story of two young girls who came to the Catholic Worker seeking shelter. They were turned away due to overcrowding, and one of them froze to death. The other found her way back to the Catholic worker and became a part of the ministry. In the busyness of ministry, Day failed to see how troubled this young girl was. As Day and her team were caring for new arrivals, the young girl killed herself in the upstairs bathroom.

The movie captures the pain Dorothy Day felt. In the film, her community turns against her, insisting that she stop accepting mentally ill individuals, drug addicts, and prostitutes. Shortly thereafter Day is attacked by a drunken guest and beaten. Rather than eject the perpetrator, Day embraces her. This act of self-sacrificial love for the broken reawakens the community to its call to live as Christ, no matter what the cost.

I expected Dorothy Day to have answers that had somehow eluded me, but instead I encountered a woman who was able to live with the ambiguity of life; someone who was secure enough in her faith that she did not need to have all the answers to life's questions. Why did that woman kill herself? Why didn't their love for her heal her? Where had they failed? Where was God? How could they protect themselves from future failures? These are the questions most of us would have asked.

Most of us would have responded as Day's community responded—by closing the door, locking out the dangerous people, and protecting ourselves from future pain. But Day does the opposite, opening the door wider, exposing herself to greater pain, refusing to retreat, silently shouting a cry of resistance.

After Shelly's suicide attempt, my community responded much the same way that Day's had done. I invited Shelly to stay with my family, and I and began a three-month fight with my board of directors to allow Shelly to move into a little house located on our property. Members of my board feared the worst would happen, Shelly would hurt herself, or someone else on our property and the ministry would be liable. There were some that felt we should not welcome those with substance-abuse issues into the ministry but should instead focus on those with less severe issues.

I dug in my heels and won the battle, but it was costly. I lost two board members who had been solid supporters, and I also lost myself. Somehow Shelly's success became the means by which I would measure my own success. I had not been able to rescue my father, and though I did not realize it at the time Shelly became my second chance. I became very protective of her, and I allowed myself to become blind to the dangers ahead.

Within six weeks of winning the fight to have Shelly live on site, she relapsed and returned to her heroin addiction. She refused to enter a treatment program, and I was forced to ask her to move out of the house. It almost killed me. To this day she will not speak to me, and this has caused one of the deepest wounds I carry.

Like Dorothy Day, sometimes those seeking to do good simply get beaten up. Once again I wanted to quit: to crawl back to my suburban world and pretend this hellish place of addiction and death did not exist. This agonizing experience forced me to admit my own limitations and to learn more about addiction and mental illness. It was at this time that we began working with the men from The Healing Place, a 198-bed residential recovery com-

> *This agonizing experience forced me to admit my own limitations and to learn more about addiction and mental illness.*

munity boasting one of the highest recovery rates in the nation. Men from The Healing Place began serving in the furniture bank, and they became my wisest teachers. They restored the hope I had lost and helped me to recognize my own limitations.

I wish I could say that through this painful experience I finally decided to take my pastoral-care professor's advice and develop healthy boundaries. But it would take a few more beatings before I finally learned that lesson, largely because my friends from The Healing Place were watching out for me and keeping me from sliding back down that slippery slope of enabling.

The issue of mental illness among the homeless population is well documented. Depression, bipolar disorders, schizophrenia, post-traumatic stress disorders, and codependency are the most common mental-health challenges we have seen in our client interactions. Recognizing that I lack the skills and training to effectively minister to individuals with addiction and severe mental illness, I have developed partnerships with substance-abuse treatment facilities and mental-health providers in our community. Unfortunately, mental-health services are difficult to access, and many of those who most need the services refuse to seek treatment, or do so sporadically. Those who do find treatment often take themselves off their medications as soon as they feel better, only to return to their original state. Mental illness is the underlying cause for much of the chronic homelessness we see in our community, but it often masked by substance abuse.

In the movie *The Soloist*, a well-meaning journalist befriends Nathaniel, a mentally ill, homeless man. In frustration he lashes out at the director of the day site for homeless folks, saying, "I want you to help him because he is sick and he needs medication and you have a team of doctors here. Tell him to sit down with them. Isn't that what you are supposed to do?"

The director looks around the room and responds, "Look at these people; every one of them have been diagnosed more than you can imagine and as far as I can tell it has not done them any good."

The director goes on to say, "Nathaniel has one thing going for him right now—a friend. If you betray that friendship, you destroy the only thing he has going in this world."

That comment struck me as the wisest advice that could be given to anyone working with individuals who suffer from mental illness: be a friend, and also learn to receive the friendship of others.

I am honored to call Charles Fitzgerald my friend. Charles has become a wise counselor to me and has helped me gain a better understanding of substance abuse and recovery. Over the years I have witnessed many of my friends relapse time and time again. In those times when I most wanted to give up, it was Charles who gave me hope in the fact that God can help even the most longtime addict find healing.

Insights from Charles Fitzgerald

I started using drugs at age sixteen and was in active addiction until I entered The Healing Place at the age of forty-nine. During that time, I tried different ways to change my lifestyle. I decided I did not want to shoot dope no more, but I still wanted to smoke crack, hang out, and drink. So I went into treatment for dope, never realizing that everything else would lead me back to the same place. Or I would decide to give up using all drugs but still wanted to hang out, sell drugs, hook up with the girls, and go to parties—not realizing that that lifestyle could not be separated from using.

I realized that I could not buy drugs with the intent of selling them, because I had become my own best customer. One thing a guy told me that helped was, "A monkey can't sell bananas." I can't sell drugs. So to support my habit, I started stealing drugs from the drug dealers I was working for. I have had people kick my door in and put a gun to my head and say, "Why should I let you live?" The insanity of the disease makes you think you can just take the drugs, and no one will notice. When you are caught up in the addiction, you do some crazy things.

When I hear stories of a woman leaving her children for three and four days and running off to go get high, I can relate to that woman. I understand her. I understand why she would leave the house to get one hit, and I understand how when she ran across someone like me, who would offer her more and more if she would stay with me and trick herself out, and she would do it. I would hold women hostage because their addiction made them my slave.

The core of my disease is that I am selfish and self-centered. Addicts only care about "What is in it for me?" Late in my mom's life, she had Alzheimer's. I would run people through the house and tell her that they were a cousin she did not remember. I left people in the house with her, not thinking about her safety, or what they would do to her. It was all about me. I went through my life blaming people: my mom, my brother, the rest of the world. When I stole stuff, I thought, "They don't have a right to lock me up." I never thought about those I stole from.

I finally got sick and tired of being sick and tired. I had taken over my momma's house after she died and turned it into a crack house. Things were disappearing out of my house, and I was sleeping on a couple of mattresses on the floor. People just came in and out and did whatever they wanted. I was lying there one night thinking, "Why am I living like this? No lights, no water, I'm dirty, I'm stinky." And I thought, "If I have to live like this, I might as well be dead."

The Healing Place took me in when I had nothing. When my family cast me out, they took me in and did not ask for a dime: they just asked me to change. After completing The Healing Place program, I met Wendy. The first time I met her, she gave me a computer and was asking me about my schoolwork, and I thought, "She don't really care. She just drumming up conversation." Then I said, "Can I get a chair too?" and Wendy gave me a chair too. That is when I realized that all these people had been giving me help. I realized it was time for me to start giving back. I now realize that the more I give, the more others are willing to come on board and give too.

I now live in Highland Park, the neighborhood I grew up in, the neighborhood that I did my running in. I see the same people still out there, and I just say, "I don't do that anymore." I don't mean to put them down, but I hope that eventually they will realize they don't have to live that way either.

I never would have chosen to volunteer had I not met Wendy. In serving others, I realized it is not about me, it is about me making a way for other people. Getting involved at Embrace taught me that a lot of people do care about people like me. It is just that people like me that are still out there are closed off, and think that people don't really care. But I had to open up my heart and open up my vision in order to really see. I try to get people who are stuck in their addiction to open up their minds and realize that people really do care.

I try to get people who are stuck in their addiction to open up their minds and realize that people really do care.

In Shelly's situation, she did not have a recovery network; she was not working a recovery program. A strong network is very important. All addicts need someone who can understand what they are going through, and who will hold them accountable. It is wonderful to have people like Wendy around, who care, but it is not enough.

Networking and sponsorship is the key to my staying clean and sober. I stay in meetings, so I hear people talk about the crazy things they have done. I call my sponsor when I wake up in the morning and feel like all hell is about to break loose, and he will remind me to do a ten-step inventory. I keep people in my life who help me see things the way they really are. My disease is always trying to trip me up by feeding me lies.

After three years, my disease still comes at me real crazy. It does not matter how far down the road you are, the disease still creeps into our lives and tells us we are failing and falling. It tells us that we aren't anything anyway, so we might as well use. It lies and says, "There ain't nothing good in your life." But if I stop and take an inventory, I realize the good in my life. I look at where I was before I got clean: homeless, no clothes, hungry; and then I look at where I am today: in school, living in a nice house, employed. And it teaches me gratitude and silences my disease. If people do not work the twelve steps, stay connected to a strong network, and go to meetings, then they will fall prey to the disease. It is always out there, and it will creep in at the craziest time.

What I have learned is that addiction is a feelings disease. I do a lot of the things I do because I just don't like what is going on with me. So I use my drugs and alcohol to make me feel better and help me forget about that problem. But when I come down, that problem is still there. So the only way I can get rid of the problem without actually facing it is to get high again.

When someone goes into treatment, gets cleaned up, then things start looking a little better. But then the feelings come back, and you think, "I know I am in treatment, and things seem to be getting a little better, but I just don't feel good." So I think, "If only I had a girl who would hold me and hug me and make me feel good, then everything would be OK." The relationships become a replacement for the high of the drugs; it makes you feel good for a short time. So then you just shut the world out, and the relationship becomes an obsession, and no one goes to work or takes care of the kids; they just try to keep feeling good. The other person becomes my focus instead of my recovery, and I am in trouble.

The process teaches me that I have to replace all those feelings and outside issues by getting closer to God, so I can feel, "I'm OK; right where I am, I'm OK." I don't need something from the outside like the drugs, the house, the girls, the cars to make me feel good. I am who I am, and I am OK.

But we always want the quick fix, the girl who will make me feel good. But then when the girl wakes up and realizes she don't like me, and I have not developed a network of people and a strong recovery program, and I have not gotten closer to God, then I am left with hurt feelings, and the drugs that can fix it are just on that next corner.

Throughout all the AA [Alcoholics Anonymous] and NA [Narcotics Anonymous] literature, we are taught to find a God of our understanding. That worked for a man like me because I was totally against the church. My momma dragged me there as a kid and made me go; she threatened to beat me if I did not go. What really kicked me was that after [her] being in the church for almost fifty years, the pastor refused to preach at her funeral unless he was paid three hundred dollars, so he did not show up at her funeral—that after her years of faithful service.

Before I went to The Healing Place, I did not think there was a God. It is just something people run around shouting about. But when I look at my past, and I remember the guy that I was out popping pills with, that lost his mind, or the guy I was out running with who got shot and killed right next to me, and here I am, I came back. I know it was not anything that I did that protected me. I now know there is a God, because I keep waking up every morning when I should be dead. I ask myself, "What if there is a God, and I don't figure it out until I get to the gate?" I decided it is better to have a God and not need one than to need a God and not have one.

When I was in The Healing Place, the director said, "If you miss the spiritual part of the program, you miss the program." I started creeping out of the building in the early morning and getting down on my knees and prayed, "If there is a God, please show yourself to me." I did not have a raincoat or a jacket, and I started to notice that the rain would start when I went into the building and stop as soon as I left the building. At first I thought I was going crazy. So I asked my friend to watch the weather with me and let me know if I was crazy, or if God got me. He said, "Man, you right. The rain does stop every time we walk out the building. God does have you."

So every morning, I roll out of bed, hit my knees and pray. I thank God for another day and thank Him for keeping me out of the way so I can be the vessel that carries the message of hope that He uses to help others come to know Him. As I grew in the AA fellowship, I learned to pray. It taught me to feel comfortable in the church again. I am now comfortable in any church, because I know God. I now go and speak in Catholic churches with a white woman, and I am feeling comfortable. Back before I knew God you would never be able to convince me that one day I would speak in a Catholic church with a white woman!

In the AA fellowship, I am taught to free myself. I learned that it does not matter what anyone thinks of me, God's opinion is the only one that matters. I think a lot of the mental illness is caused when people are not willing to free themselves. They hide the things they have done and refuse to tell anyone, and it makes them sick. When I was able to free myself and trust others with my se-

> *When I was able to free myself and trust others with my secrets and my sick thoughts, I found the healing I needed.*

crets and my sick thoughts, I found the healing I needed. That is what the third, fourth, and fifth steps are all about.

So many people try to hide from their addiction. Some hide in the church because they know no one will know when they mess up. I need someone just like me standing beside me holding me accountable. Drugs and alcohol change the way we think. I need someplace where I can share all the messed-up stuff going through my mind. If I shared in a church the stories of the things I done, ya'll going to cast me out. If I told you I slept with the deacon's wife, and I share my story, you would cast me out. But in an AA or NA meeting, I can share what is really going on with me, because they had those thoughts too. No one will judge me. I can share openly and not be criticized or cast out because of it.

I don't go to AA meetings for me. It is not about me anymore. I go for those coming behind me. Now a lot of people are watching me and make sure I keep going to my meetings. I never want anyone to say, "Well, Charles does not go to his meetings, so why should I?" It is not about me anymore. I show up for others so others keep coming back and they have hope. It's about us setting the tone for others. I set a tone of, "I don't play." I take recovery seriously. Unless people are willing to work the program and willing to accept help, there is nothing you can do to help them.

I met Wendy right after one of her ladies relapsed and wanted to give up. I started getting into what Wendy was doing, and I realized that it takes a lot of courage to do what she does. That is why I do what I do, because of people like Wendy. The future of Embrace was right there, but she did not stop, she did not give up. That is why I am doing this. It is people like Wendy that produce people like me. Wendy does not know it and does not see it, but if she had not been there, I would not be where I am.

Charles's dream: To help those in recovery overcome the barriers they face to long-term stability and bring hope to those who feel defeated and forgotten.

---

16 When Dreams Collide

The secret to success lies in how great organizations mobilize every sector of society— government, business, nonprofits, and the public— to be a force for good . . . Great organizations work with and through others to create more impact than they could ever achieve alone.

—LESLIE R. CRUTCHFIELD and HEATHER MCLEOD GRANT

The furniture-bank component of our ministry continued to grow quickly and was consuming all my energy. My desire was to build a holistic ministry meeting the physical, emotional, and relational needs of families in transition, but meeting this one physical need for furniture had become the only thing I had time for. I could not continue to grow the furniture component and remain faithful to my call. Our community needed a true furniture bank, but I knew that I was not the executive director for the job.

I shared my dilemma with Karen Stanley, who serves as the executive director of both CARITAS (www.caritasshelter.org), the largest emergency shelter in Richmond, and The Healing Place (www.thpva.com), the 198-bed residential recovery program mentioned in the last chapter. Karen is one of the most respected and skilled executive directors in Richmond. She recognized the value of the furniture-assistance program and offered to approach her board about absorbing the furniture bank into CARITAS.

Karen also had a dream: a dream of moving CARITAS beyond emergency assistance to programs designed to help clients stabilize. Karen recognized that 25 percent of those served by her agencies would be homeless again within a year. The most difficult time faced by homeless clients is in the first few months after they exit the shelter, and Karen knew that few had the resources needed to furnish their new homes. CARITAS partners with over 190 congregations across the metro Richmond region, and she knew this could fuel the increase in furniture donations needed to take the furniture bank to the next level.

Karen also had dreams for the men graduating from The Healing Place. As I shared my desire to preserve the "pay-it-forward" culture of Embrace Richmond, and my desire to eventually give the operation away to the homeless population, she immediately recognized how this vision fit into her dream of creating transitional employment opportunities for the graduates of The Healing Place. Using the furniture bank as an employment-training opportunity would not only help The Healing Place men make the transition back into independent living; it would also provide the labor needed for the furniture-bank expansion. It was a win-win situation all round.

What I feared would be the death of my dream became the catalyst for something neither of us could have seen apart from one another. In September 2008, CARITAS absorbed the furniture-bank component of Embrace, freeing me to focus on the relational, spiritual, and emotional health of those being served by emergency shelters.

In the fall of 2008, Embrace Richmond received our first AmeriCorps grant. Working collaboratively with CARITAS, we developed a transitional-employment program through which we hired graduates of The Healing Place to work in the furniture bank. My dream of giving the furniture ministry away to the homeless population that birthed it was finally realized. But there was one more dreamer needed to fulfill the vision: Karen O'Brien.

Five years earlier in our Yada Yada group, Karen O'Brien had shared her vision of trucks carrying stuff from suburban communities into urban communities. During those five years, Karen had owned and operated an appliance company, gaining warehousing, retail, and management experience. With the severe economic conditions of 2008, Karen and her husband were forced to close their business. As I was searching for my replacement, Karen O'Brien was seeking a new path. I still have to pinch myself every time I see Karen out in the warehouse directing traffic. God had been preparing her to take what Stephanie had inspired, and what I had birthed, and grow it into a self-sustaining program that would live on beyond all of us.

Though I thought letting go of the furniture program could possibly be the end of my ministry, I found it to be the beginning. I learned that dreamers cannot fly alone. The Yada Yadas helped me birth my dream, countless numbers of homeless men and women helped shape the dream, the fellow dreamers from The Bridge helped propel the dream, and CARITAS and The Healing Place helped me reclaim my dream. I wish that earlier in my journey I would have sought to work more collaboratively. Through this collaboration, I came to see God at work in other organizations both secular and faith-based. Together our dreams form a beautiful tapestry, each complementing and strengthening the other.

The mistake I made in trying to work independently is one that I see many organizations make, particularly faith-based organizations. Eric Swanson, in "Ten Paradigm Shifts toward Community Transformation," points out that "The Bible is replete with examples of how God used secular people in partnership with his people to fulfill his purposes. Think of Joseph and Pharaoh, Nehemiah and Artaxerxes, Esther and King Ahasuerus."[1] A common misconception among leaders of faith-based nonprofits is that collaborating with secular agencies or receiving federal funds will lead to the watering down of the faith elements. I have found the exact opposite to be true. By partnering with secular and government agencies, we were able to leverage our resources toward meeting the emotional and spiritual needs, by allowing the secular agencies to meet the physical and economic needs. Over the years, we developed a number of partnerships with faith-based, governmental, and secular agencies. The key to community transformation is recognizing that all the assets of a community are God's assets, and learning to bring these assets together for the common good. It requires a level of humil-

> *The key to community transformation is recognizing that all the assets of a community are God's assets, and learning to bring these assets together for the common good.*

1. Swanson, "Ten Paradigm Shifts," 8.

ity and a willingness to trust others to do those things you are not called to do. That trust is built over time through relationships. I am thankful that when I was a new executive director, Karen Stanley took the time to get to know me as a person, listened to my dreams, and was willing to allow her resources and Embrace Richmond's vision to align with her own in a way that has given life to a beautiful collaborative effort.

Interview with Karen Stanley

I found my way onto the CARITAS board of directors because of my role as the domestic-violence coordinator for the Chesterfield County Police Department. In that role I was seeing families become homeless due to domestic violence. Shortly after I joined the board, CARITAS was approached by the United Way about developing a family program because of the growing number of families seeking emergency shelter. Prior to this time, starting in the late 1970s, CARITAS worked exclusively with singles, and predominantly with single men. We started as a winter cots program, operating only in the coldest months of the year. But in the mid-'90s this increase in the number of families seeking shelter resulted in what is now our Family Focus program. I became the executive director of CARITAS in 2000, and we have continued to grow as the demand for emergency shelter has increased. All our programs now operate year-round, with an increased number of sites open during the winter months. CARITAS is the largest emergency-shelter provider in Richmond, partnering with 190 congregations.

CARITAS's family program is unique because we have always embraced the whole family while other shelters focus exclusively on women and children. CARITAS is the only emergency-shelter program that allows the fathers to stay with the family and welcomes single fathers with children. CARITAS is also the only family shelter that accommodates families with teenage children. Our program was designed to meet these gaps in the existing homeless-services system.

I think CARITAS has a tremendous advantage over traditional shelters because of the hope, faith, and care provided by our congregational host sites. The love and hospitality extended by the congregations far outweigh the disadvantage of having to move the clients from site to site.

When working with congregations, we help them understand that we are showing our faith by doing what we do—by sheltering, feeding, and caring for those in need. We help the congregations understand that our guests may be coming from different faith traditions. Some are Jewish, Muslim, or have other or no religious faith. We ask that our host sites respect our guests and their faith tradition and to refrain from proselytizing among our clients. However, the host sites are free to offer religious activities, such as Bible studies or worship services, to our guests as long as the activities are optional and offered in an area apart from the room where the clients are being sheltered. Many of our clients do participate actively in the life of the host congregation, attending choir practice, praying at meals, or attending Bible studies. As long as religious teachings are not forced upon the client or made mandatory as a condition of shelter, the congregations are free to offer faith-oriented activities to our clients.

CARITAS does receive government funding. The way I understand the role of religious components and government-funded programs is that faith elements of a program must be optional, and government funds cannot be used to support religious activities. That is the only limitation. While it is a government requirement, it is also a respect issue. I would never want to force anyone, especially people in crisis, to participate in religious activities against their will simply so they can receive the basic necessities of life. That would simply be wrong.

When I joined CARITAS, Homeward—the coordinating agency for homeless services in Richmond—had already started working with homeless-services providers to try to work more collaboratively. Over the years, we have seen a decline in some of the turfism, and the spirit of collaboration has continued to grow between providers. Once a month, all the executive directors from all the homeless-services agencies get together for lunch to figure out how we can all work better together instead of trying to do things on our own. These lunches have fostered relationship building. Once you develop a personal relationship with someone, it is far easier to pick up the phone if you have a problem or a concern or an idea of how to work together on a project.

A lot of the turfism and lack of collaboration from the past was driven by funding concerns—each agency's trying to protect their piece of the pie. Funding shifts, particularly government funding trends, have shaped much of our current system. Back in the 1980s the federal funding was going toward emergency shelter, and we saw an increase in the number of emergency-shelter beds. Then in the 1990s the shift was away from emergency shelter and toward transitional shelter. At that point we saw a decrease in the number of emergency-shelter beds, as a number of agencies abandoned emergency-shelter programs and developed transitional programs. It was at that point that CARITAS committed to become a year-round program because of the drop in emergency beds in the system. At this time we are experiencing another shift: this time away from transitional shelter programs and toward permanent housing.

While CARITAS does receive some federal funds, we are not heavily dependent on government support. This has allowed us to be responsive to the needs in our own community and to fill the gaps in our existing system. Homeward, in partnership with all of the larger homeless-services agencies, worked very hard to evaluate our current system and to develop the "Ten Year Plan to Prevent and End Homelessness." Some key directives came out of that plan. We realized as a system that we needed to change the way we do business. Rather than putting all our resources into emergency and transitional shelters, we needed to put more of our resources toward those programs and services that worked best across the country; programs which result in permanent, affordable housing, and programs that prevent homelessness. Being a team player, I felt that my obligation was to pass that message on to my board. We had to think how CARITAS might reinvent itself if it were to help fill these gaps.

CARITAS mobilizes thousands of volunteers from over 190 congregations. Our volunteers are a tremendous asset, and I did not want to lose that investment as we made this shift. That is why the furniture-bank program was such a great fit. It was a way of engaging congregations, individuals, and families who had not been able to get involved in the shelter side of CARITAS but could nonetheless host a furniture drive or volunteer in the furniture bank.

It has been a year since CARITAS absorbed the furniture bank from Embrace Richmond, and we have been very successful in getting our congregations to support this new venture. We now have a furniture drive going on somewhere in the city every week of the year.

I also love walking into the warehouse and seeing the guys from The Healing Place working in the furniture bank. They say, "Hi, Mrs. Karen!" with a big smile and are so happy to be working over there, giving back and staying sober. I am so thankful. Some of them just need a little extra time and a safe place where they get the support they need to continue to work their recovery. The furniture bank has become an extension of the community they find at The Healing Place. It is close enough that they can come to The Healing Place for lunch and see the other guys and hang out with their peers and work in an environment where they are supported.

The next phase in this shift toward long-term stability is to focus on the employment needs of our clients. We are starting by helping the clients with special talents find employment through social-enterprise ventures such as home repair; but ultimately we hope to start a staffing company that will offer employers that layer of protection, and shelter them from liability that they are so concerned about when hiring convicted felons. If we can reduce the risk to the employer, we are hoping employers will give our clients a chance to prove themselves. With CARITAS's 190 congregational partners and the thousands of volunteers, we are confident that we will be able to find employers who will hire our clients. The congregations are always asking "What more can we do?" and this will allow us to say, "Hire them! Don't just give them a roof over their head for a week, but give them a way of providing for themselves and surviving on their own, long-term." So it is not just a message to employers but to our extensive volunteer base. We need people who can help our clients network, prepare resumes, work on getting their GED, overcome transportation barriers, and prepare for interviews.

CARITAS did not come up with these plans in isolation; we have always worked within the system trying to fill the gaps, partnering with both the faith community and secular agencies to determine our unique role in helping to prevent and end homelessness in our city.

Karen's dream: To open The Healing Place for Women in Richmond, and to develop an employment program that will help clients move from emergency shelter to long-term stability.

---

17 Little Dreamers with Big Visions

Never doubt that a small group of thoughtful, committed citizens can change the world; indeed, it's the only thing that ever has.

—MARGARET MEAD

Freed from the responsibilities of the furniture bank, I spent months praying, seeking God's direction on where Embrace Richmond was to go from there. God has showed us many things over the years, but the most significant is that Embrace is called to "equip and empower the saints for works of service": all the saints, from the homeless men and women in the shelter to the housewives in the suburbs.

To end homelessness, we have to stop the revolving shelter doors. To achieve this goal we have to focus attention on the communities where the majority of our clients were moving; public-housing projects and low-income communities. We turned to the wisdom of John Perkins and the power of our own story to envision a means of strengthening these communities. Perkins's book *Beyond Charity: The Call to Christian Community Development* offers this ancient Chinese poem as an illustration of true community development:

> Go to the people
> Live among them
> Learn from them
> Love them
> Start with what you know
> Build on what they have:

But of the best leaders
When their task is done
The people will remark
"We have done it ourselves."[1]

Perkins emphasizes the importance of raising up leaders from the community and empowering them to bring about change, in a way similar to the way Stephanie became the catalyst for the furniture ministry. Perkins writes, "Programs and services benefit a local community only to the degree that they come from the 'bottom up,' that is, reflect the actual felt needs of the people being served . . . If programs and services are done *for* a community, rather than *with* and *by* the people of the community, these programs do not help the people of the community develop."[2] This vision of empowering indigenous leaders is the key principle behind the way we do ministry. Rather than focusing on the needs of the at-risk communities, we focus on the gifts; seeking out people with dreams of making a difference. In the beginning, as we found the dreamers, we partnered with congregations and nonprofits to bring their dreams to life, and invited those moving into the communities out of the shelters to join in the effort. This methodology not only brings about positive community change but provides a means of empowering leaders and of providing care for those in transition.

I moved from seeing myself as the executive director to seeing my primary role as that of a dream releaser. But empowering indigenous leaders is not enough; we need to connect the dreamers with the resources and leadership skills of others from across the city. We began a training program called Unity Works, to educate both urban and suburban dreamers about how to do ministry together in an urban setting. In our first session of Unity Works, God sent one of the most beautiful women I have ever met, Tammy McClure. Tammy came to Unity Works in response to God's call on her life to serve the poor. As I watched Tammy take hold of the principles of Christian community-development, I saw her listening with great openness to the men and women from the streets of Richmond who told her of their God. In those encounters, Tammy began to see that God was far bigger and far more powerful than

1. Quoted in Perkins, *Beyond Charity*, 35
2. Ibid., 103

142

she had ever imagined. My greatest joy was seeing Tammy present her dream: she dreamt of being a bridge builder, helping others to cross over the boundaries of race, class, and geography, and to come to see a God that is so much bigger than our safe, suburban world typically allows. Through Unity Works, God has helped dozens of dreamers discover their dreams and has provided a support system to help them begin living their dreams. We believe Unity Works and the dreamers it is unleashing will transform at-risk communities and congregations alike.

The church needs the poor and the poor need the faith community; together both are transformed and it is through this transformation that we will begin to see "Thy kingdom come on earth as it is in heaven."

Ironically, this movement into at-risk areas began with the gift of a

> *The church needs the poor and the poor need the faith community; together both are transformed and it is through this transformation that we will begin to see "Thy kingdom come on earth as it is in heaven."*

four-bedroom house in Highland Park, which was donated by a graduate of our Unity Works program. Embrace Richmond returned to its Highland Park roots, using the house initially to house AmeriCorps members, then to house chronically homeless individuals, and ultimately as a hospitality house. When the house was first offered, I was uncertain what to do with it. I asked my team to give me ideas, and Charles Fitzgerald shared that he had been dreaming of having a house for people in recovery, particularly for those with mental-health issues.

Charles is a clown, but he was serious when he said, "They need to see that no matter how crazy you are, you can overcome it all. No one is more crazy than me! I used to be on tons of medications and have been diagnosed with every mental illness possible, but I have made it, and so can they." Charles not only defeated his addiction but has completed a certificate program in substance-abuse counseling and is on the dean's list at our local community college, working on a bachelor's degree in human services. Charles is one of our key leaders in our Unity Works training and has inspired many dreamers.

Following Perkins's advice, we decided to be strategic in providing aftercare support to those exiting the shelter system. We started with weekly prayer walks in communities with a high concentration of formerly homeless families, then visited these families and listened to the challenges they were facing. The first of these communities was Hillside Court. Hillside, which is located adjacent to our warehouse facility, is one of the smallest Richmond Redevelopment Housing Authority (RRHA) housing projects and offered us an opportunity to experiment with community-development principles taught by the Christian Community Development Association (CCDA). The proximity of our ministry center to this neighborhood, and the fact that we were residents of that community and thus have a vested interest in its success, gave us the ability to build strategic partnerships with the schools, the RRHA housing manager, and—most important—the residents of Hillside Court. We began by simply visiting the families that were receiving assistance from the furniture bank. We started building relationships, praying with them, and listening to their hopes and dreams. Since its inception, Embrace Richmond had served dozens of residents of Hillside. People had come to know us as people who help other people, and this foundation was crucial to building trust and authentic relationships with our new friends.

Early on in our Hillside visitation, I became aware that one woman who had come to Embrace to serve, at the invitation of a friend years earlier, lived in Hillside. Mrs. Mildred had served faithfully at Embrace but had stopped coming due to a lack of transportation. Though it had been years since I had seen Mrs. Mildred, she immediately embraced my new team and me. When we asked Mrs. Mildred what her dreams for her community were, we learned that she had been serving on the tenant council and that they had wanted to start a clothing closet there in the neighborhood. Hillside is located in a largely industrial area, and there are no clothing stores within walking distance. Mrs. Mildred became our first Hillside dreamer and together helped start Embrace Hillside. We formed our community-based ministry around the mission of blessing Hillside in whatever way God directed, through the Hillside residents. Allen Hirsch in his book *The Forgotten Ways* notes that "the most vigorous forms of community are those that come together in the context of a shared ordeal or those that define themselves as a group with a mission that lies beyond themselves—thus initiating a risky journey . . . During this shared ordeal, the initiates move from being disoriented and individualistic to developing a bond of comradeship and communality forged in the testing conditions."[3] Hirsch points out that "this is exactly how Jesus does discipleship: he organizes it around mission. As soon as they are called he takes the disciples on an adventurous journey of mission, ministry, and learning. Straightaway they are involved in proclaiming the kingdom of God, serving the poor, healing, and casting out demons. It is active and direct disciple making in the context of mission."[4]

Seeking to be a blessing to Hillside was indeed a risky venture. In a community riddled with crime and poverty, this group of largely single mothers and grandmothers have banded together to actively show love for their neighbors, who are very often also their enemies. It is the most beautiful expression of the gospel message that I have ever seen. Currently Embrace Hillside helps distribute clothing to the residents on a monthly basis, gathers together on a weekly basis to pray and encourage one another, and weekly serves together in the community in whatever way they are needed. The team is led by dreamers like Mrs. Mildred, and we are simply their support system. We are the logistics behind her army of laborers which consists of formerly homeless women, many unemployed, who desperately need income, but who choose to give of themselves to help others. We were now home, back where we began, empowering dreamers who in turn mobilize their communities. Tammy McClure serves as the missional bridge builder for the Hillside community, helping others find their way out of the pew and into mission in the city.

Interview with Tammy McClure

I grew up at Smith Mountain Lake in southwest Virginia. I became a Christian as a child, but in my high school years I stopped going to church. It was when we had children that we realized the importance of doing things the right way and knew we needed to be back

3. Hirsch, *The Forgotten Ways*, 221.
4. Ibid., 120.

in church. Over the years, I became very involved in the life of the church. On a mission trip to Mexico, I first experienced poverty. I came back looking for local missions, realizing we have poverty thirty minutes down the road in the inner city of Richmond. I was your typical suburban mom, doing suburban mommy things, but God was saying to me, "There is more." I knew there was more, but I just did not know what.

Last year God took me into a desert. It has been the most painful and lonely year of my life. As I cried out to God to speak to me, God led me to Jeremiah 2:7 [NIV]: "I brought you into a fertile land to eat its fruit and rich produce. But you came and defiled my land and made my inheritance detestable." When I read the passage, I was so confused. I could relate to being in a fruitful land and enjoying its bounty, but I could not figure out how I could have defiled God's land. So I cried out to the Lord, asking, "God, how have I disappointed you? I have been faithful in attending church, I have taught Sunday school, worked with the youth groups, served on committees and women's Bible studies. How has this defiled your land?" And the Lord so clearly impressed upon me this: "Tammy, you are giving me your Christian resume, but things are not as you see them. You do not see what I see, and what I see is what matters. I see someone who is half full of me and half full of self. I do not need a Tammy McClure, I need an empty vessel."

During my time in the desert, I again heard God calling me to the inner city of Richmond to spend time with the "least of these." I had the desire to serve, but it was really hard figuring out where I fit in, and that is what Unity Works helped me with. It was the open door I was searching for. Unity Works was so key; because being out here in the suburbs, we really have no idea what the urban context is like. We don't know who is doing what, and we lack that network into the urban communities. The Unity Works program gave me the broader understanding of homelessness and poverty that I needed.

For suburbanites like me, the urban setting is much like the foreign missions setting; in a lot of ways it is a different culture. One example of this was at Thanksgiving. We had LaKisha, one of the women I met through Embrace, and her boys over for Thanksgiving dinner, and she was eating green-bean casserole and was saying, "Oh my goodness! What is this? I love this! What is it called?" I had just assumed everyone had turkey, dressing, and green-bean casserole for Thanksgiving dinner. I asked her what her traditional Thanksgiving dinner was and she said, "Chitlins, macaroni and cheese, and collard greens." I know that when I say "Thanksgiving" out here in my suburban world, everyone automatically thinks, "Turkey, stuffing, mashed potatoes, pumpkin pie, and cranberry sauce"; but what I realized was that when I say "Thanksgiving dinner" to my urban friends they could be thinking, "Chitlins, macaroni and cheese, and collard greens." This is just one example of a cultural difference that most people do not even realize is there. Sometimes we are not speaking the same language.

Unity Works helped me see the big picture and realize that my experience and culture were very different than [the experience and culture of] those living in the inner city. It also helped me see that neither was good or bad; they are just different. Just like with foreign missions, we need cultural training.

I was also taught through Unity Works to follow the same guidance of foreign missionaries by looking for the "person of peace" in the communities where we are serving, recognizing that we are called to be colaborers with the leaders within the community, and not to come in with our own agenda.

The most powerful element of Unity Works was when we had to draw our dreams on a poster board. I have never been asked to do that and realized I didn't know how to dream like that. I prayed over my dream board for weeks and I had no idea what to draw, but then God gave me the vision of a bridge. Even after I finished Unity Works, it took nine months for that bridge to be built and for me to really start living that dream. You have to wait on the Lord to bring about our dreams. God does have a plan. It is His plan that we leave our places of comfort and go to the "least of these." Scripture commands us to be missionally engaged. It is not that we say, "I am going to do 'this' for God," but more God saying to us, "Here is my will for you. Will you

> *I think that is the power in dreaming: it is not a human effort but more us opening ourselves up to what God has for us.*

walk in it?" I think that is the power in dreaming: it is not a human effort but more us opening ourselves up to what God has for us. I have never been asked to dream like that before . . . never. That was big!

While I was in Unity Works, I volunteered with Homeward during their Project Homeless Connect, where they pull together all the homeless services in the city into one place. They offer things like dental care, haircuts, eye care, clothing and shoes, etc., so that the homeless individuals can come to one place and have all their needs met. My job at this event was to be a navigator—helping one homeless person navigate through all the services. I had a lot of fear and anxiety about this event and about who I would be paired with.

On the day of the event, I was paired with an older man in his sixties named Lewis. I spent the day with Lewis and really enjoyed his company. Toward the end of the day, Lewis was given a new pair of boots. He sat down in a chair and put his foot out sideways and strained to reach his feet but he could not. He shared that he had back problems and could not bend over. So I got down on my knees and I helped him remove his shoe and put on his new boots. I can't really explain what happened in that moment. I felt this wave of the spirit wash over me, and I heard in my heart, "You are sitting at the feet of Jesus." It was so significant, and I felt time had stopped in that moment. Later that day, Lewis was sitting in the barber's waiting area, and I walked over to him, and only for a moment there was something in his eyes that took my breath away: a sparkle, a brightness, a twinkle of something in that man's eyes, and I knew I was looking into the eyes of Jesus. I felt like he was saying, "Yes, you do see me, and you are in the right place." I had been walking in a desert searching for the Lord, and he met me there in that moment. I know this may sound crazy to many people, but I promise you on November 20, 2008, a day I will never forget, I sat at the feet of Jesus and looked into his eyes through a homeless man.

Yesterday I was sharing with a woman from Hillside Court, where I now minister, that I had spent a year in the desert, and her response blew me away. She said, "You have been to the desert? Isn't it the most beautiful place? When you are in the desert, it is only you and God." She was a desert dweller; she knew where I had been. I promise you when you come out of the desert and you look back, you will see just how beautiful that place is.

I have a heart for the suburban church, the people in the pews are my people; they are me. I just needed someone to build that bridge for me so I could follow God. I want to build that bridge now for others. I am in such a place of peace right now. My heart is no longer restless; it is not searching any more. It is where it is supposed to be. I have no idea where my bridge-building efforts will lead, but it does not matter, because I know that God has called me to be right where I am.

When I gather with my friends in Hillside Court, I am always amazed by how God is working, and how clearly I see God working through the people I am meeting. Just the simple fact that we are together is a miracle, because we simply are so rarely united the way we are. The world had separated me from my impoverished friends, but somehow the spirit has bonded us together

> *The world had separated me from my impoverished friends, but somehow the spirit has bonded us together and there is a power in that unity.*

and there is a power in that unity. When we are together you just feel the Spirit, because it is a supernatural gathering that only God could bring about.

A few weeks ago, one of our ladies witnessed a robbery and stabbing outside her apartment. That event shook me to the core, but it made me realize that I have always been in a safe place. My ministry was always in the church, in the safety of my own community. I have never had to rely on God this way, and the Scriptures have really come alive for me through this. When I was doing ministry in the church, the Scriptures did not have the power they have to me now, because I was not really relying on them, I was not walking them.

But now I am walking by faith, unlike anything I have ever done. It is almost like I am a new Christian, and I am reading these passages for the first time. They are so relevant to my life now. For example, putting on the "armor of God" takes on a different meaning when I am visiting in Hillside after a stabbing than it had when I was just sitting in the pews of the church. One passage that has really spoken to me in this work is Psalm 91, which speaks of finding protection and refuge under the wings of God. That passage has a whole new meaning in a place where there is real danger.

In our suburban churches, we are not taught how to live with this kind of faith. My urban friends have become my teachers. I watch them and am challenged by the richness of their faith, that has been formed through great hardship. My urban friends live by faith because they have to. The richness of their faith just seems to pour out into me. I have learned so much from them.

It is hard to describe where I am spiritually today. In a way, my faith has been simplified. It is like I am a new Christian who has just fallen in love with the Lord all over again. I cannot even compare where I am now to where I was before I began this journey. I have seen God so at work since I have stepped into the inner city—more in the past year than in all my years in church. I have seen God in so many places, doing so many things, that somehow it has allowed me to just rest and relax in His presence. I don't have to figure it out, or try to understand the theological implications of what is going on. I just have to recognize that God's got it, and everything becomes so much simpler.

When I first came through Unity Works, I was questioning, "Where is Jesus in this?" And I now realize that He is in all of it. That has been a journey for me: coming from a conservative-evangelical church background. I have come to realize that we are the gospel; we carry it with us where ever we go. When we go, people know we are there because of our faith, and the Lord will provide the opportunities for people to see God.

I have been particularly moved by the times we have spent in prayer. There is nothing like a room full of faithful black women in prayer! We have to take our understanding of sharing our faith out of the box that we were taught to carry it in, and trust the Holy Spirit. I have such peace in all this because I know I am where I belong, and God has the rest. I thought initially God wanted me to go into the inner city to "share Jesus," but I have been blown away by the spirit of Christ that I have encountered. So much of what we call faith in the suburban world has stopped with our minds and does not make it into our hearts until we learn to walk it and live it the way our urban friends have done.

Every month when we do our community Blessing Day, we gather in a circle and pray for the community, and every month the circle gets bigger, more diverse. My hope is to one day see that circle grow to embrace the whole community: black, white, rich, poor, young, and old—all gathered to pray for the community.

While I was in the desert, I had to ask myself, "If Jesus lived my life, what would my life look like? Who would I be with, and what would I be doing?" My heart has found its home! I have learned about walking by faith and not by sight, waiting on Him because His timing is perfect in all things. I learned what it means to fulfill the first and second greatest commandments the Lord his given us; to love. I have surrendered myself to the Lord to follow wherever he leads, living my faith through action by the power of the Holy Spirit. I am so in awe that the Lord has allowed me to see and participate in a small way in His work at Embrace. I believe He has great things ahead!

Tammy's dream: To see Hillside Court become a beacon of light and hope for all—both for its residents and for those who come across the bridge from the churches.

---

18 Dreams for the Church

*We will have to repent in this generation not merely for the vitriolic
words and actions of bad people, but for the appalling silence of the
good people.*

—MARTIN LUTHER KING JR.

Amid such great human suffering, both domestically and abroad, I find
the church consumed with its own comfort and preservation. Most pastors would agree with Allen Hirsch's observation in *The Forgotten Ways*
that "too much concern with safety and security, combined with comfort and convenience, has lulled us out of our true calling and purpose."[1]
We spend all our resources building our own Christian "kingdoms,"
where we focus the majority of our resources on the needs of our own
congregants and fail to see the church universal, and as a result God's
kingdom is divided into millions of small isolated townships ruled often
by self-interest and ego. I fear the future of the church in America will
follow the path of Highland Park UMC: turning inward, ignoring its
missional call, and ultimately dying a slow death.

As a church we have often separated ourselves from those who are
suffering from poverty, and pass judgment much the way Job's friends
judged his suffering—as the result of some human sin, a separation from
God, the result of something done by the one who suffers. I have a love/
hate relationship with the book of Job. I love it because it is a clear message from God that all suffering is not the result of human sin. I also

1. Hirsch, *The Forgotten Ways*, 25.

hate the book of Job because God allows human suffering. God allows Job to be tested, God allows the forces of evil to take everything from Job simply because the devil wants to prove a point. In the end, it proves to be a poor gamble on the part of Satan, because Job will not deny the goodness of God. Even after everything is lost, Job still believes in God. He still claims that God is on his side. He refuses to take the blame; he refuses to become the cause of his suffering. Like Via, Phyllis, LaKisha, and Charles, Job refuses to be defeated. Job teaches us that suffering is not a punishment from God but rather a tool for molding and shaping us into the vessels of God.

Suffering is not primarily the result of a spiritual failure on the part of the one who suffers. Suffering just is. The answer to human suffering is not that "they need to 'find' Jesus," but more often that "we need to 'find' Jesus in them." I do not deny human sin or the consequences of it. Obviously those who choose to use drugs bring much suffering upon themselves, and this is a huge part of the suffering that I have witnessed. However, others suffer great injustice through no fault of their own.

When we think about suffering at the level of the individual, it becomes clear that we cannot condemn the poor for being poor. However, in practice our actions as the church say something different. When a church invests millions in a building campaign but does not give even a tithe of their offerings to the poor, what does this say about what we think about the poor? When a church spends more time building programs for its congregants who live in luxury instead of addressing substandard housing or unemployment, what message are we preaching? Have we forgotten that as Christians we should seek to consistently embody the life, spirituality, and mission of our founder Jesus?

I spent ten years serving in the local church prior to moving to Richmond, but today I find myself with those on the outside looking in through their eyes, and what I see grieves me. Shane Claiborne writes, "Only Jesus would declare God's blessing on the poor rather than on the rich and would insist that it's not enough to love just your friends. I began to wonder if anybody still believed Jesus meant those things he said. I thought if we just stopped and asked, What if he really meant it? it could turn the world upside-down."[2] Claiborne also writes, "I wondered

2. Claiborne, *The Irresistible Revolution*, 41.

what it would look like if we decided to really follow Jesus. I wasn't exactly sure what a fully devoted Christian looked like, or if the world had even seen one in the last few centuries. From my desk in college, it looked like some time back we had stopped living Christianity and just started studying it."[3] Richard Stearns, in his book *The Hole in Our Gospel*, reminds us that "it's not what you believe that counts; it's what you believe enough to do."[4] The challenge in front of us is to put down our theology books and start really living our faith.

> *Much of our theologizing has led us to overspiritualize the human condition, often focusing on an afterlife where all suffering will end as a way of avoiding the pain of the suffering we see all around us.*

Much of our theologizing has led us to overspiritualize the human condition, often focusing on an afterlife where all suffering will end as a way of avoiding the pain of the suffering we see all around us. Stearns speaks to this issue:

> Focusing almost exclusively on the afterlife reduces the importance of what God expects of us in this life. The kingdom of God, which Christ said is "within you" (Luke 17:21 NKJV), was intended to change and challenge everything in our fallen world in the here and now. It was not meant to be a way to leave the world but rather the means to actually redeem it . . . Those words from the Lord's prayer, "your kingdom come, your will be done on earth, as it is in heaven" were and are a clarion call to Jesus' followers not just to proclaim the good news but to *be* the good news, here and now. This gospel—the *whole* gospel— means much more than the personal salvation of individuals. It means a *social revolution.*[5]

I have written this book in part as a guide for individual Christians, like myself, who want to get off the consumer-driven hamster wheel, and who desire a life filled with true meaning and divine purpose. But it

3. Ibid., 71.

4. Stearns, *The Hole in Our Gospel*, 87.

5. Ibid., 17, 20 (italics original).

is also for congregations who desire to raise up radical Christ followers who have the courage to live radically sold-out lives. We are the body of Christ, called to bring good news to the poor, to set the captives free, to offer sight to the blind, and to declare the year of the Lord's favor (see Luke 4:19). We should love kindness, do justice, and walk humbly (see Micah 6:8). Like Moses, we are to lead God's people out of poverty and oppression to the Promised Land—not only for the sake of the kingdom that is to come, but because of God's kingdom that is already here—the one that we the church should be ushering in together: the kingdom that offers hope to the hopeless and healing to the broken, that celebrates the reign of God on earth.

This book is not intended to be a step-by-step, how-to guide on becoming a faithful Christian. Jesus already gave us that. He hung out with the least, the lost, and the outcast. He cared more about us than himself, and he was willing to sacrifice everything to make a way for God's kingdom to come on earth. He calls his disciples to join him in what he already started. It is simple: we are to feed his sheep, love one another, and strive to be one true body of believers. But it is also very hard: we are to allow Christ's perfect love to cast out all the fear that binds us to our places of comfort and complacency, and to allow his Spirit to open our eyes so that we may see his presence in the poor and the outcast. Jesus has called us to the poor not only to ease their suffering but also to transform us into his likeness. In their suffering we see Jesus, and through their perseverance we gain the boldness to live as Christ.

> *Jesus has called us to the poor not only to ease their suffering but also to transform us into his likeness.*

Where should you start? Alan Hirsch, in *The Forgotten Ways*, affirms my own experience: "In the study of the history of missions, one can even be formulaic about asserting that *all great missionary movements begin at the fringes of the church*, among the poor and the marginalized, and seldom, if ever, at the center." He goes on to state, "It seems that when the church engages at the fringes, it almost always brings life to the center."[6]

6. Hirsch, *The Forgotten Ways*, 30 (italics original).

Hirsch reminds us that "the movement that Jesus initiated was an organic people movement; it was never meant to be a religious institution."[7] Dr. Martin Luther King's prophetic works in his "Letter from Birmingham Jail" remind us of the danger of turning the church into an institution: "I have been so greatly disappointed with the white church and its leadership . . . All too many have been more cautious than courageous and have remained silent behind anesthetizing security of stained-glass windows . . . The contemporary church is a weak, ineffectual voice with an uncertain sound. So often it is an arch-defender of the status quo . . . But the judgment of God is upon the church as never before. If today's church does not recapture the sacrificial spirit of the early church, it will lose its authenticity, forfeit the loyalty of millions, and be dismissed as an irrelevant social club with no meaning for the twentieth century. Every day I meet young people whose disappointment with the church has turned into outright disgust."[8] King was echoing the sentiments of Mohandas Gandhi, who said, "I like your Christ, I do not like your Christians. Your Christians are so unlike your Christ."[9]

Most would agree that King's prophecy has come true in our own time. The church has been dismissed by many "as an irrelevant social club with no meaning." Will we continue to focus on our own needs for comfort and security, or will we choose to follow Jesus beyond the borders of our comfort zones and see him in those we have written off as socially unacceptable?

Many are seeking to find fresh expressions of the church and to cast a vision for the church of the future, but few have seen it. What does it look like? It looks like the Yada Yadas dreaming together, like Aileen and Via learning to be family across racial and socioeconomic lines. It looks like heroin addicts and housewives stuffing couches into cars for recently homeless families. It looks like Charles, a formerly homeless addict, creating a healthy home for mentally ill, homeless men. I see it in the streets of Highland Park, being reclaimed from an age of ruin. I see it as Becky stands in solidarity with LaKisha and fights for justice. I hear whispers of it around the boardroom tables as secular and faith-based groups join together to be a blessing to their cities instead of guarding their own

7. Ibid, 54.

8. King, "Letter from Birmingham Jail."

9. Brainy Quotes, "Mohandas Gandhi Quotes."

territory. I witness it as Rosalind and others like her die to their own self-interests in an age of entitlement and serve others. But most powerfully, I see it as Mrs. Mildred gathers the lost sheep of Hillside Court together every week to feed one another, and in unity to turn and feed the hurting world all around them. That is what the church looks like when it seeks to simply follow Jesus. It is not flashy or sophisticated, but it holds more power than any force in history. It looks very much like Jesus, gathered with Mary and Martha in their living room, sharing, teaching, and loving those around him.

I finally found it! I found the intersection of the needs and dreams of a community, the calling and capacities of the church, and the mandates and desires of God for a community. And it is the most beautiful thing I have ever seen. I believe it is the church of the future and the greatest hope we have of breathing new life into the Body of Christ.

19 The Wounded Dreamer

*But a changed world requires change agents, and change agents
are people who have first been changed themselves.*

—RICHARD STEARNS

As I have made this journey, I have come to realize that dreamers are not
born but made, often through pain and suffering. You will find brokenness at the core of all those who contributed to this work. What sets the
dreamers apart is their willingness to allow their pain to bring healing to
others. Henry Nouwen, in *The Wounded Healer*, writes: "It seems necessary to re-establish the basic principle that no one can help anyone without becoming involved, without entering with his whole person into the
painful situation, without taking the risk of becoming hurt, wounded or
even destroyed in the process . . . The great illusion of leadership is to
think that man can be led out of the desert by someone who has never
been there. Our lives are filled with examples which tell us that leadership asks for understanding and that understanding requires sharing."[1]

Until I sat down to write this story, I did not see how it was my own
brokenness and pain that led me to take each of the steps in my journey.
I never realized how, despite my own reservations, God truly can use all
things for good, if only we allow our ashes to be transformed into things
of beauty. Henri Nouwen writes of his journey as a minister:

> In the middle of all fragmentation one image slowly arose as the
> focus of all considerations: the image of the wounded healer. This

1. Nouwen, *The Wounded Healer*, 72.

image was the last in coming. After all attempts to articulate the predicament of modern man, the necessity to articulate the predicament of the minister himself became most important. For the minister is called to recognize the suffering of his time in his own heart and make that recognition a starting point of his service . . . Thus nothing can be written about ministry without a deeper understanding of the ways in which the minister can make his own wounds available as a source of healing.[2]

My hope and prayer in sharing my story and the story of others I met along the way is that the stories will bring hope to others who find themselves either at the beginning of a journey, seeking which direction to go, or stranded on the side of the path, feeling lost, alone, and defeated. I have stood at both places many times, and in those times rather than quit or retreat, I wish I would have recognized that my missteps and falls were as important as my successes, for they led me to greater understanding.

The death of my father opened me up to hearing God's call, and the pain of Shelly's relapse helped me see my own limitations. Finding God's path for our lives is never simple and is often painful. As my own journey shows, it is seldom a straight shot but more often a wandering, meandering trail. I think that is why I love the labyrinth so much. It is a wonderful metaphoric display of a life spent in pursuit of God and of the journey to then carry that wisdom out into the world. Life is full of twists and turns, but God is always dwelling in the middle of what seems like chaos and disorder. When we reach that center and take the time to sit and listen, we will hear the answer to our deepest questions. We simply must be willing to ask those questions, and then be ready to enter in when God opens the doors of discovery.

> *Life is full of twists and turns, but God is always dwelling in the middle of what seems like chaos and disorder.*

While my story has come to an end, this is not the end of my journey. I believe it is just the beginning.

My prayer is that God grant us peace and hope. I pray that God will raise up an army of hope bearers who will bring hope to the hope-

2. Nouwen, *The Wounded Healer*, xvi.

less as we come together and share both our pain and our dreams. For those of you to whom God has already given a dream, I pray you find the courage to live it. For those of you who are already pursuing your dreams, I pray that God will surround you with fellow dreamers who will help you persevere. And for those of you who have yet to discover your God-given dream, I pray that you allow God to take you to places of pain and to transform them into a source of hope for others. For those who have never endured deep suffering, I pray you will enter into the pain of others and walk in solidarity with those who suffer, taking on their pain and allowing God to teach you through them. Listen to their stories and embrace them as your most valued teachers.

20 Lessons from a Dreamer

Vision without action is merely a dream. Action without vision just passes the time. Vision with action can change the world.

—JOEL BARKER

I set out on my journey to find a community of faith that sought to make a real tangible difference in the world. Rather than discover that community, I had the privilege of birthing such a community. It is a community made up of many wounded healers who, like me, are seeking a way of life that offers more than fortune and fame. A community that seeks a way to live true to the calling placed on our lives and birthed from our pain. It is not a community that claims to have all the answers but instead one that is willing to ask the hard questions and to live with the ambiguity of life that often offers no answers.

From Via and Aileen I learned the power of boundary crossing and the courage to reach out to those who are different from me and in so doing to discover new sisters and brothers. From the Yada Yadas I learned that we all have dreams—dreams of making this world a better place for all God's children. From Anita, Frances, and Phyllis I learned that Christian hospitality is desperately needed in a world of broken people, and often is practiced best in places outside the church walls. From William and John I learned the harsh reality facing those who are mentally challenged and the need for meaningful work among those who face barriers to employment. From Stephanie I learned about the transforming power of giving for those who are often on the receiving end of charity. From the community of Highland Park and Mr. Tony Brickhouse, I learned that every community, no matter how impoverished, has hidden treasures: saints who desire to serve their neighbors. From Reverend Nottingham and Martha Rollins I learned that much of the desperation and poverty that we encounter in the inner city are the continuing effects of slavery and racism. From Charles I learned the importance of a strong recovery program and the power of a good network. From Sylvia and my friends from The Bridge network I learned that I am not crazy, and that God has used pain to break others out of complacency and indifference, and to move them to action. It was Patricia who showed me my own hypocrisy and inspired me to live sacrificially. From Rosalind I learned of the many snares and traps that await the poor and hold them in poverty, and from Maria, LaKisha, and Becky I learned about systemic injustice and the power of advocacy. From Rosalind and Georgiana I learned the importance of combating the spirit of entitlement. And from my own father and Shelly I learned about hopelessness and depression, and discovered its ability to steal joy from the rich and poor alike. From Karen I discovered the power of *we* through collaboration, and Mrs. Mildred helped me regain my hope and a vision for the church of the future.

Any one of these stories could easily be a book in itself. The point is not to arrive at a neat set of principles and practices that promise to fix all the ills of the world. Rather, I hope these stories help to broaden our vision of what it means to be a Christ follower and our understanding of the call of the church in the world. I share this story not to emphasize the destination or the place at which we have arrived but to accentuate the importance of the journey.

> *I share this story not to emphasize the destination or the place at which we have arrived but to accentuate the importance of the journey.*

Had the journey been taken in another city by a different pilgrim, the final portrait would look very different. We all shape and are shaped by others and by our own experiences. I do not believe there is one way of following Christ. Throughout my journey I sought the wisdom of Eric

Swanson, John Perkins, Barbara Elliott, Shane Claiborne, Christine Pohl, Richard Stearns, Gordon Cosby, Allen Hirsh, Martin Luther King Jr., and many others. While their insights were helpful to me, these could never replace the lessons I learned from the people in my own community.

The journey is not over. God continues to bring new saints into my life who are shaping our city and the ministry of Embrace Richmond. You can follow this unending story at www.wendymccaig.com where we will continue to share the dreams of our urban friends and the suburban dreamers who are crossing over the bridge. I invite you to join us on this adventure and share your hopes, dreams and desires with us. Have you discovered the place where the needs of your community meet your own God-given dreams? Do you see God moving in new and exciting ways by uniting people across racial, socio economic, geographic, and religious boundaries? Please share your stories with us and allow us to learn from your journey.

What follows is a snapshot of the programs that grew out of our journey so far. They are neither all-encompassing nor complete and unchanging. Every person who enters our ministry shapes it and informs it. However, the following principles have formed our foundation:

- True hospitality is always reciprocal, transforming both the giver and the recipient.

- Everyone has a gift to give and a dream to fulfill.

- Out of our broken places God can bring healing and hope to a broken world.

- Complacency can only be overcome through relationship with the poor.

- Entitlement can only be overcome through meaningful service to others.

- Working collaboratively expands the effect of our services and unites our city.

The following programs were birthed through this journey:

The Furniture Bank: Now operated by CARITAS, the furniture bank has value not because of the amount of furniture distributed but rather because of who is distributing it. The furniture bank employs formerly homeless individuals, who run the warehouse and deliver the furnishings; hundreds of volunteers from all sectors of the Richmond community support the furniture bank.

The Community Works program: A grassroots community-development program that identifies and equips community leaders who desire to bless their neighbors. These leaders along with leaders from area congregations work together to facilitate community-based missional small groups that address needs of impoverished neighborhoods. All the ministries birthed out of our Community Works program are led by community-based leaders.

The Just Works Program: A transitional employment program restoring dignity and hope to homeless and at-risk individuals as they help strengthen impoverished communities and assist others who are transitioning out of homelessness.

The Faith Works program: Through Faith Works, Embrace Richmond coordinates short-term urban missions experiences. The goal of these events is to educate and engage local congregations in urban ministry through hands-on service events.

The Unity Works program: An urban-missions training program that offers opportunities for people of faith to learn about the issues facing homeless and at-risk individuals in our city, and that assists them in discerning how they can help their urban neighbors who are in need.

The Dream Works program: A mentoring program that pairs "encouragers" with formerly homeless or at-risk individuals for short-term and long-term mentoring. The goal of this program is to introduce people of faith to the practice of hospitality; the program equips and teaches them to provide emotional, relational, and spiritual support that individuals in transition need in order to become all God created them to be.

All our programs are relational, and all bring together communities of wealth and poverty. Through all these programs we seek to practice hospitality and to do justice by empowering our participants to take control of their own lives and communities. All our programs seek to call those of means out of their places of comfort and complacency toward compassion and to move those taught an attitude of entitlement to give to others. All our programs happen in partnership with congregations and dozens of local nonprofits. You can learn more about Embrace Richmond at www.embracerichmond.org.

Bibliography

Brainy Quote. "Mohandas Gandhi Quotes." http://www.brainyquote.com/quotes/authors/m/mohandasgandhi_2.html/.

Campolo, Tony, with stories by Bruce Main. *Revolution and Renewal: How Churches Are Saving Our Cities*. Louisville: Westminster John Knox, 2000.

Claiborne, Shane. *The Irresistible Revolution: Living as an Ordinary Radical*. Grand Rapids: Zondervan, 2006.

Day, Dorothy. "Dorothy Day on Love: The Mystery of the Poor." *Catholic Worker*, April 1964. Reprinted in *Houston Catholic Worker*, May-June 2006.

Hirsch, Alan. *The Forgotten Ways: Reactivating the Missional Church*. Grand Rapids: Brazos, 2006.

King, Martin Luther, Jr. "I Have a Dream." Address delivered at the Lincoln Memorial, Washington DC, August 28, 1963. Online: http://www.americanrhetoric.com/speeches/mlkihaveadream.htm/.

———. "Letter from Birmingham Jail, April 16, 1963." Online: http://www.mlkonline.net/jail.html/.

Moore, Beth. *Breaking Free: Making Liberty in Christ a Reality in Life*. Nashville: LifeWay, 1998.

National Coalition for the Homeless. "Who Is Homeless?" Fact sheet. July 2009. Online: http://www.nationalhomeless.org/factsheets/who.html/.

Nouwen, Henri J. M. *The Wounded Healer: Ministry in Contemporary Society*. Garden City, NY: Doubleday, 1972.

Jones, F. Overton, and Edgar J. Nottingham III, compilers. *Highland Park United Methodist Church: A History*. n.p., 1983.

Payne, Ruby, et al. *Bridges out of Poverty: Strategies for Professionals and Communities*. Highlands, TX: aha! Process Inc., 2001.

Perkins, John M. *Beyond Charity: The Call to Christian Community Development*. Grand Rapids: Baker, 1993.

Pohl, Christine D., *Making Room: Recovering Hospitality as a Christian Tradition*. Grand Rapids: Eerdmans, 1999.

Rhodes, Michael Ray, director. *Entertaining Angels: The Dorothy Day Story*. DVD. Produced by Gateway Films. Distributed by Vision Video, Burbank, CA, 2002.

Stearns, Richard. *The Hole in Our Gospel*. Nashville: Nelson, 2009.

Swanson, Eric. "Ten Paradigm Shifts toward Community Transformation: How Churches Are Impacting Their Communities with the Good Deeds and Good News of the

Gospel." International Coalition of Workplace Ministries. Online: http://www
.icwm.net/articles_view.asp?articleid=1395&columnid/.

Wilkinson, Bruce, with David and Heather Kopp. *The Dream Giver*. Sisters, OR:
Multnomah, 2003.

Wright, Joe, director. *The Soloist*. Produced by DreamWorks Pictures and Universal
Pictures present in association with StudioCanal and Participant Media, a
Krasnoff/Foster Entertainment production in association with Working Title
Films. Produced by Gary Foster and Russ Krasnoff. Screenplay by Susannah Grant.
DVD. Hollywood, CA: Paramount Home Entertainment, 2009.